The UNOFFICIAL VIRGIN RIVER COOKBOOK

A DELICIOUS COLLECTION *of* RECIPES INSPIRED *by* YOUR FAVORITE SMALL-TOWN CHARACTERS

DAHLIA CLEARWATER

SKYHORSE PUBLISHING

Copyright © 2023 by Hollan Publishing

Skyhorse Publishing books may be purchased in bulk at special discounts for sales promotion, corporate gifts, fund-raising, or educational purposes. Special editions can also be created to specifications. For details, contact the Special Sales Department, Skyhorse Publishing, 307 West 36th Street, 11th Floor, New York, NY 10018 or info@skyhorsepublishing.com.

Skyhorse® and Skyhorse Publishing® are registered trademarks of Skyhorse Publishing, Inc.®, a Delaware corporation.

Visit our website at www.skyhorsepublishing.com.

10 9 8 7 6 5 4 3 2 1

Library of Congress Cataloging-in-Publication Data is available on file.

Design by Melissa Gerber
Photos used by permission of Shutterstock.com

Print ISBN: 978-1-5107-7474-2
eBook ISBN: 978-1-5107-7501-5

Printed in China

CONTENTS

• AT THE BAR 47 •

• FROM THE BAKERY TRUCK 89 •

WELCOME
to
VIRGIN RIVER!

With its breathtaking scenery, heartwarming stories, and jaw-dropping drama, Virgin River has become a home away from home for millions of viewers. It's no wonder—fresh air, good friends, and true love are easy to come by in this charming northern-California town. And incredible food is waiting for you at every bar, barbecue, and bakery truck.

The Unofficial Virgin River Cookbook is here to help you relive the show's most memorable moments and mouthwatering meals. Enjoy a bit of baked brie and backgammon with Muriel and Doc (page 11); curl up by the fire with Jack, Mel, and a perfectly seared steak (page 65); and let yourself be surprised and delighted by Preacher's delicious harvest salad (page 74). Just make sure you top it all off with a slice of Paige's signature apple-pear pie (page 127). In Virgin River, there's no problem pie can't solve!

This delicious cookbook is so much more than a connection to your favorite fictional town and an excuse to binge-watch *Virgin River* all over again. Full of timeless recipes for classic comfort foods, farm-to-table favorites, and sweet treats to share with family and friends, it will become a well-worn reference in your collection. So dig in and enjoy!

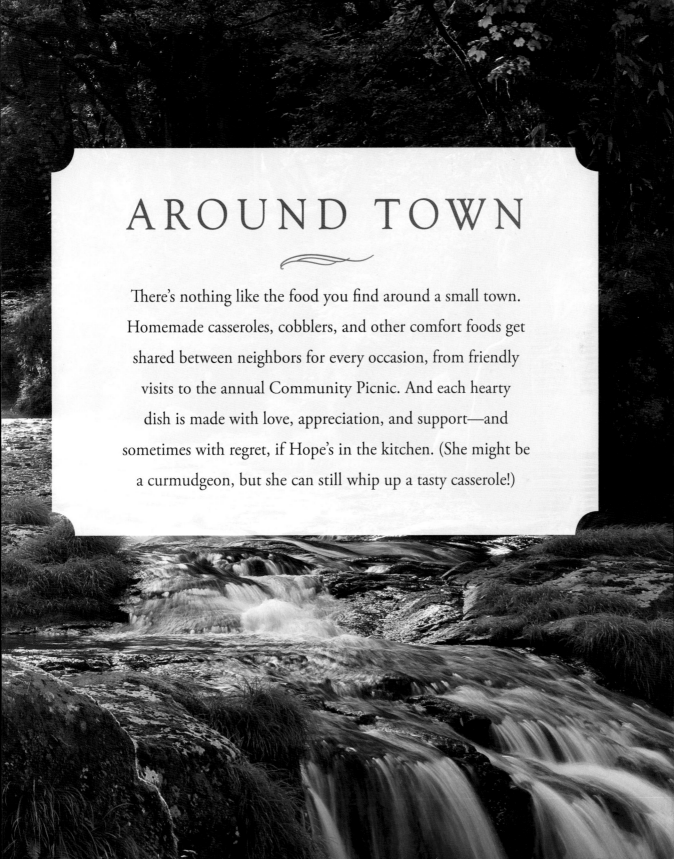

AROUND TOWN

There's nothing like the food you find around a small town. Homemade casseroles, cobblers, and other comfort foods get shared between neighbors for every occasion, from friendly visits to the annual Community Picnic. And each hearty dish is made with love, appreciation, and support—and sometimes with regret, if Hope's in the kitchen. (She might be a curmudgeon, but she can still whip up a tasty casserole!)

SWEET WAY TO WAKE UP PANCAKES

>>>>>>>>>> <<<<<<<<<<

Mix things up like Mel does by adding a little chocolate to your morning. Homemade pancakes are always a sweet thing to wake up to after an especially lovely date (whether or not your suitor spends the night). And they're super simple to whip up, which means the only thing you need to worry about is whether you're craving semi-sweet or dark.

Serves 4

1 cup all-purpose flour
1 tablespoon sugar
2 teaspoons baking powder
¼ teaspoon kosher salt
1 large egg
1 cup chocolate milk
2 tablespoons canola oil
½ teaspoon vanilla extract
¼ cup miniature semisweet or dark chocolate chips
Butter (optional)
Maple syrup (optional)
Whipped cream (optional)

1. Add the flour, sugar, baking powder, and salt to a large bowl and stir to combine. In another large bowl, whisk together the egg, milk, oil, and vanilla. Stir the wet ingredients into the dry ingredients just until moistened (being careful not to over stir), then fold in the chocolate chips.

2. Preheat a lightly greased griddle or large pan over medium heat.

3. Pour the batter ¼ cup at a time onto the hot griddle. Let each pancake cook until the batter begins to bubble and the bottom is golden brown, then flip it and continue cooking until the other side is equally golden.

4. Top finished pancake stacks with more chocolate chips, butter, maple syrup, and whipped cream, if desired.

HARD-WORKING OATMEAL

➤➤➤➤➤➤➤➤➤ ⫷⫷⫷⫷⫷⫷⫷⫷

CHARMAINE WILL BE THE FIRST TO TELL YOU THAT CREATING LIFE IS HARD WORK, and food is fuel. These easy (and stomach-settling) overnight oats are fully customizable and can keep in the fridge for up to five days so they're ready when you need them. Add a teaspoon of honey or maple syrup for sweetness if you need it.

Serves 2

1 cup rolled oats
2 cups favorite milk
Pinch of sea salt
4 tablespoons chia seeds
1 large banana, sliced
1 cup fresh (or thawed frozen) blueberries
Other optional toppings: chopped dates, nuts, seeds, cacao nibs, or shredded coconut

1. Divide the oats, milk, and pinch of salt between two bowls and stir to combine. Cover the bowls with plastic wrap or a lid, and let them chill in the refrigerator overnight.

2. The next day, top each bowl with chia seeds, sliced banana, blueberries, and any other toppings that sound good to you.

RECOVERY POTATO SOUP

>>>>>>>>>> <<<<<<<<<

LIZZIE BECOMES QUITE THE COOK BETWEEN SEASONS THREE AND FOUR! Hope may turn up her nose at eggs after her accident, but she wouldn't dare refuse the young baker's creamy potato soup. A bit of smokey ancho chili powder makes it irresistible.

Serves 6

6 strips bacon, chopped
3 tablespoons unsalted butter
1 medium yellow onion, chopped
3 cloves garlic, minced
⅓ cup all-purpose flour
6 large gold potatoes, peeled and diced
4 cups chicken broth
2 cups whole milk
⅔ cup heavy cream
1 teaspoon kosher salt
1 teaspoon freshly ground black pepper
¼–½ teaspoon ancho chili powder
⅓ cup sour cream, plus more for serving
Shredded Cheddar cheese, for serving
Chopped scallions, for serving

1. Place the bacon in a large pot over medium heat and cook until crisp and browned. Remove it from the pot and set it aside, leaving the fat in the pot.

2. Add the butter and onion to the pot and cook over medium heat until the onions are tender, 3 to 5 minutes. Add the garlic and sauté it until fragrant, about 30 seconds.

3. Sprinkle the flour over the onions and garlic and whisk it until no lumps remain.

4. Stir in the potatoes, broth, milk, heavy cream, salt, pepper, and ancho chili powder to taste. Bring to a boil over medium-high heat and cook until the potatoes are tender, about 10 minutes. Reduce the heat to a simmer.

5. Using a ladle, carefully transfer half of the soup to a blender and puree. (For a smoother consistency, blend all of the soup in batches or use an immersion blender.)

6. Pour the pureed soup back into the pot and stir in the sour cream and most of the bacon, reserving some for garnish. Simmer for about 15 minutes.

7. Ladle the soup into bowls and garnish with sour cream, bacon, Cheddar cheese, and scallions.

TAKE A BREAK
WITH BAKED BRIE

→→→→→→→→→→ ←←←←←←←←←←

WHEN A BIT OF BRIE AND BACKGAMMON SEEM SURPRISINGLY CIVILIZED TO YOU LIKE THEY DO TO DOC, you might need a break from the more demanding people in your life. Top this one with candied walnuts for an even more refined treat.

Serves 6 to 8

8-ounce wheel double cream Brie
2 tablespoons honey
A few sprigs fresh rosemary
Crusty French bread or crackers, for serving

1. Preheat the oven to 350°F.

2. Remove the cheese from its packaging and place in a small oven-safe pan. Drizzle with about half of the honey and sprinkle with half of the rosemary leaves, stripping the leaves from the stem.

3. Bake for 10 to 12 minutes, or until the cheese is soft in the center and the honey is bubbling. Remove from the oven and let cool for a few minutes.

4. Transfer the Brie to a serving platter or serve from the pan. Drizzle with the remaining honey and sprinkle with the remaining rosemary. Serve with crusty bread or crackers.

GOURMET GRILLED CHEESE

>>>>>>>>>> <<<<<<<<<

THE "FAMOUS GRILLED CHEESE" LIZZIE OFFERS RICKY AS INCENTIVE TO STAY PROBABLY ISN'T ANYTHING SPECTACULAR, but this one is. Rustic bread and marinated vegetables make all the difference. Take it to the next level by pairing it with your own homemade focaccia (see Focaccia for a Midday Surprise on page 81).

Serves 4

3 large ripe tomatoes, cut into ¼-inch-thick slices

1 medium red onion, thinly sliced

3 tablespoons red wine vinegar

Kosher salt and freshly ground black pepper

4 pieces focaccia bread or other rustic bread, halved horizontally

1 tablespoon mayonnaise

8 ounces thinly sliced mozzarella

3 cups arugula, coarsely chopped

Olive oil, for pan-frying

1. In a large bowl or baking dish, layer the tomatoes and onion. Pour over the vinegar and sprinkle with salt and pepper. Let everything marinate at room temperature for 30 minutes, then drain the tomatoes and onion and pat them dry with paper towels.

2. Open up the focaccia slices and spread mayonnaise on one or both sides. On one piece of bread, place a layer of mozzarella, then add slices of tomato, a few onions, and some arugula, then another layer of mozzarella. Place the other slice of bread on top.

3. Heat the olive oil in a wide skillet and fry the assembled sandwiches in batches, pressing on the tops using a spatula to flatten the sandwiches and keep the fillings together. Fry the sandwiches until each side is golden brown and the cheese is melted. Alternatively, use a panini press to press the sandwiches according to the manufacturer's instructions.

ANYTHING BUT ARUGULA SALAD

→→→→→→→→→→ ←←←←←←←←←←

IF YOU SHARE HOPE'S HATRED OF ARUGULA, this creamy Caesar salad is just the ticket. Homemade croutons and dressing make this dish worthy of its place among the many other mouthwatering offerings at the Moonlight Mingle.

Serves 4

FOR THE CROUTONS
3 tablespoons olive oil
1 clove garlic, minced
8 slices baguette, halved
1 tablespoon grated Parmesan cheese

FOR THE DRESSING
2 cloves garlic, minced
2 teaspoons Dijon mustard
1 teaspoon Worcestershire sauce
2 teaspoons freshly squeezed lemon juice
1½ teaspoons red wine vinegar
⅓ cup olive oil
½ teaspoon sea salt
Pinch of freshly ground black pepper

FOR THE SALAD
1 large head romaine lettuce
⅓ cup shaved Parmesan cheese

1. Preheat the oven to 350°F. In a small bowl, combine the olive oil and garlic.

2. To make the croutons: Place the slices of bread on a baking sheet, brush them with the olive oil mixture, and sprinkle them with the Parmesan. Bake until lightly golden and crisp, 10 to 12 minutes. Let them cool while you make the salad.

3. To make the dressing: In a small bowl, whisk together the garlic, mustard, Worcestershire, lemon juice, and red wine vinegar. Slowly drizzle in the olive oil while whisking constantly. Whisk in the salt and pepper, taste, and adjust the seasoning as desired.

4. To make the salad: Wash and pat dry the lettuce, then tear it into shreds and move it into a serving bowl. Drizzle the dressing over the lettuce and toss to coat evenly. Top it with the shaved Parmesan and croutons and toss again.

HEART-HEALTHY
CHICKEN STIR-FRY

→→→→→→→→→→ ←←←←←←←←←←

HOPE MIGHT PREFER HER FOODS SLATHERED IN CREAMY CHEESE, but Mel's healthy stir-fry will help her live to see the town through its next big upset. Serve this flavorful version over riced cauliflower to keep your heart as happy as your tastebuds.

Serves 4

FOR THE STIR-FRY SAUCE
2 tablespoons cornstarch
3 tablespoons soy sauce
¾ cup chicken broth
1 tablespoon honey
1 tablespoon sriracha sauce (optional)
1 tablespoon toasted sesame oil

FOR THE CHICKEN STIR-FRY
1 pound boneless skinless chicken breasts, cut into 1-inch pieces
Kosher salt and freshly ground black pepper
2 tablespoons vegetable oil, divided
1 large broccoli crown (without the stem), cut into 1-inch pieces
1 large red bell pepper, cored and cut into 1-inch pieces
3 cloves garlic, minced
1 tablespoon peeled and finely minced ginger
1 teaspoon red pepper flakes (optional)

1. To make the sauce: In a small bowl, whisk the cornstarch into the soy sauce until fully dissolved. Add the chicken broth, honey, sriracha (if using), and sesame oil and whisk to combine. Set aside.

2. To make the stir-fry: Season the chicken pieces with salt and pepper.

3. In a large frying pan, heat 1 tablespoon of the oil over medium-high heat until shimmering. Add the chicken, spacing them apart in an even layer. (You may need to cook in batches to avoid overcrowding the pan.) Cook the chicken, turning halfway through, until golden brown on the outside and no longer pink on the inside, about 6 minutes. Transfer it to a plate, leaving the oil in the pan.

4. Add the remaining 1 tablespoon of oil to the pan and heat until shimmering. Add the broccoli, bell pepper, garlic, and ginger and fry until the broccoli is bright green and the pepper is crisp-tender, about 4 minutes. Add the chicken back to the pan.

5. Stir the sauce to combine, then pour it into the pan. Continue to cook, tossing constantly, until the sauce coats the ingredients and has thickened slightly, 1 to 2 minutes.

CHICKEN POT PIE
IN A PINCH

→→→→→→→→→→→ ←←←←←←←←←←←

FIND SOME PEAS STASHED IN YOUR FREEZER BY A BEGRUDGING HEART PATIENT LIKE MEL DOES? Quickly turn them into the ultimate country comfort food, chicken pot pie, using a rotisserie chicken. (Just keep an extra bag handy in case of injuries.)

Serves 6

4 cups chicken broth
1 bouillon cube
½ cup (1 stick) unsalted butter
1 medium onion, finely chopped
2 large carrots, cut into ½-inch rounds
1 large rib celery, sliced
3 tablespoons chopped chives
2 cloves garlic, minced
Kosher salt and freshly ground black pepper
½ cup all-purpose flour, plus more for dusting
¼ cup heavy cream
3 tablespoons dry sherry
1 (2-pound) rotisserie chicken, shredded
1 (7-ounce) bag frozen pearl onions
1 (9-ounce) bag frozen peas
1 (14.1-ounce) package pie crusts
1 egg beaten with 1 tablespoon water

1. Preheat the oven to 375°F. In a large saucepan, bring the chicken broth and bouillon cube to a simmer over medium heat.

2. In a large pot or Dutch oven, melt the butter over medium heat. Add the onions, carrots, celery, chives, and garlic and cook, stirring occasionally, until tender. Season with salt and pepper. Sprinkle the flour over the vegetables and stir until the flour smoothly coats the vegetables and there are no lumps, about 2 minutes. Stir in the hot broth, heavy cream, sherry, shredded chicken, frozen onions, and frozen peas. Bring everything to a boil, then reduce the heat to a simmer.

3. Divide the mixture among six ovenproof ramekins or bowls, and place them on a baking sheet.

4. Dust the countertop with flour and roll out the dough to an even thickness and about 1 inch wider on all sides. Using a biscuit cutter or large glass, cut out dough circles to cover the tops of the ramekins with about ½ inch of overhang all around. Crimp the dough over the edge of the ramekins. Brush with the egg wash and make four small slits on the top using a sharp paring knife. Bake the pies for 35 minutes, until the pastry is golden brown and the filling is bubbling. Remove them from the oven and let cool for a few minutes before serving.

A MEAN CHICKEN AND BISCUIT CASSEROLE

>>>>>>>>>> <<<<<<<<<<

Using this dish as a peace offering may be the one thing Charmaine does right—no one in their right mind would slam the door on this incredible casserole. For added flavor, top raw biscuits with melted butter and a bit of garlic powder.

Serves 6 to 8

FOR THE FILLING
2 cups chicken broth
1 cup half-and-half
6 tablespoons unsalted butter
1 large onion, chopped
3 large carrots, chopped
3 large ribs celery, chopped
½ cup all-purpose flour
1 teaspoon kosher salt
¼ teaspoon freshly ground black pepper
4 cups shredded rotisserie chicken
½ cup frozen peas (not thawed)

FOR THE BISCUITS
2 cups pancake mix
⅔–¾ cup cold buttermilk
½ cup grated Cheddar cheese
¼ teaspoon dried parsley

1. Preheat the oven to 425°F. Coat a 3-quart casserole dish with cooking spray.

2. To make the filling: In a medium bowl, whisk together the chicken broth and half-and-half. Set aside.

3. In a large skillet, melt the butter over medium-high heat. Add the onion, carrot, and celery and cook, stirring, for 10 minutes. Add the flour and cook, stirring, for 1 minute. Lower the heat to medium and slowly stir in the chicken broth mixture. Cook, stirring often, until the mixture is thick and bubbly but not boiling, 5 to 6 minutes. Stir in the salt, pepper, chicken, and frozen peas.

4. Pour the mixture into the prepared baking dish. Cover with foil and bake for 10 minutes.

5. To make the biscuits: In a large bowl, stir together the pancake mix, buttermilk, cheese, and parsley until a soft dough forms.

6. Remove the baking dish from the oven, remove the foil, and stir the mixture. Drop about ¼ cup of biscuit dough at a time on top of the mixture to form about 8 biscuits.

7. Bake, uncovered, for 12 minutes, or until the biscuits are golden brown and a toothpick inserted into the center of one comes out clean.

LUMBERJACK TURKEY LEGS

⟶⟩⟩⟩⟩⟩⟩⟩⟩⟩ ⟨⟨⟨⟨⟨⟨⟨⟨⟵

EVEN THE TINIEST LUMBERJACKS CAN APPRECIATE A ROASTED TURKEY LEG. The one Christopher enjoys at the Games may be the size of his head, but he seems pretty happy with his choice. A compound butter gives these legs the deliciously crispy skin everyone loves.

Serves 4

4 turkey legs or drumsticks (bone-in, skin-on)
4 tablespoons unsalted butter, softened
1 teaspoon kosher salt
¼ teaspoon freshly ground black pepper
1 teaspoon poultry seasoning
1 teaspoon dried thyme
½ cup chicken or turkey broth

1. Preheat the oven to 350°F.

2. Use paper towels to pat the turkey legs dry, then place them in a large roasting pan.

3. In a small bowl, combine the butter, salt, pepper, poultry seasoning, and thyme. Rub the seasoned butter over the turkey legs and under the skin. Pour the chicken broth into the pan.

4. Roast the turkey legs for 1 hour and 30 minutes or until a meat thermometer reads 170°F when inserted into the thickest part. Remove the roasting pan from the oven, tent it with foil, and let the turkey legs rest for 10 minutes before serving.

HONEY-BAKED HAM JUST FOR HOPE

>>>>>>>>>> <<<<<<<<<<

HOPE IS RIGHT (AS USUAL): HONEY-BAKED HAM IS ALWAYS A CROWD-PLEASER. Although Preacher's roast pork is surely divine, this simple and scrumptious recipe can be prepped for the Mingle in minutes. Add some drama by using maple bourbon instead of water for the glaze.

Serves 8

8-pound bone-in spiral-sliced half ham
2 tablespoons unsalted butter, melted
3 tablespoons honey
1½ cups sugar
½ teaspoon seasoned salt
½ teaspoon onion powder
½ teaspoon ground cinnamon
½ teaspoon ground nutmeg
¼ teaspoon ground ginger
¼ teaspoon ground cloves
¼ teaspoon paprika
Pinch of allspice
3 tablespoons ham juices

1. If desired, trim the ham of excess fat, then place it in a slow cooker. In a small bowl, combine the melted butter and honey, then brush it all over the ham, getting into every nook and cranny and between the slices. Cover and cook on low for 4 to 5 hours.

2. When the ham is warmed through, preheat the broiler to high. Line a roasting pan with heavy-duty aluminum foil. Transfer the ham to the pan, reserving the ham juices in the slow cooker.

3. In another bowl, combine the sugar, seasoned salt, onion powder, cinnamon, nutmeg, ginger, cloves, paprika, and allspice. With clean hands, pat half of the sugar mixture over the top of the ham. Place the ham under the broiler for 4 to 5 minutes, until the topping is bubbling and caramelized. Remove it from the oven.

4. Transfer the remaining sugar mixture to a small saucepan. Add 3 tablespoons of the ham juices from the slow cooker. Bring to a boil over high heat, stirring. Boil for 1 minute, then remove from the heat.

5. Brush the glaze over the ham, then place it under the broiler again for 1 to 2 minutes, being careful not to let it burn. Let the ham rest for 5 to 10 minutes before serving.

BAKED RIBS
FOR BUSY PEOPLE

>>>>>>>>> <<<<<<<<<

SOME THINGS ARE WORTH WAITING FOR, like the romance between Jack and Mel, and Preacher's Texas-style barbecue. This easy recipe saves you the trouble of hiring help to man the smoker without sacrificing any of that slow-cooked flavor.

Serves 4 to 6

FOR THE DRY RUB
½ cup brown sugar
1 tablespoon garlic powder
1 tablespoon onion powder
1 teaspoon kosher salt
1 tablespoon chili powder
2 teaspoons cumin
2 tablespoons smoked paprika
1–2 teaspoons cayenne pepper

FOR THE RIBS
2 racks pork ribs (about 6 pounds)
One 8-ounce jar barbecue sauce

1. Preheat the oven to 275°F. Line a baking sheet with foil.

2. To make the dry rub: In a small bowl, combine all the dry rub ingredients; set aside.

3. Rinse the pork ribs and pat them dry with paper towels. Using a sharp paring knife, carefully remove the membrane from the back of the ribs. Spread the dry rub all over the ribs, covering both sides evenly. Wrap each rack tightly in foil and place it on the prepared baking sheet, meat-side up.

4. Transfer the ribs to the oven and bake for 3 hours for spareribs, 2 hours for baby back ribs, or until the meat pulls away easily from the bone when tested with a fork. Remove them from the oven and set the broiler to high.

5. Carefully open the foil over the sink and drain the liquid, then remove the foil wrapping. Place the ribs on the baking sheet and brush them with the barbecue sauce.

6. Place them under the broiler and broil for 5 minutes, brushing the ribs with more sauce as desired, until the sauce is lightly caramelized and bubbling.

7. Let the ribs rest for 5 to 10 minutes before cutting between them and serving.

HOMESTYLE BAKED MAC AND CHEESE

→→→→→→→→→ ←←←←←←←←←

YOU CAN'T BE CRANKY WHILE EATING MAC, even if you did just discover your small-town retreat is a cobweb-covered cabin. Just make sure you clean any birds' nests out of the oven before baking this creamy treat, and you'll feel your stress levels sink in no time.

Serves 8

Olive oil
Kosher salt
1 pound dried elbow pasta
4 cups shredded medium sharp Cheddar cheese, divided
2 cups shredded Gruyère cheese, divided
½ cup (1 stick) unsalted butter
½ cup all-purpose flour
1½ cups whole milk
2½ cups half-and-half
1½ teaspoons kosher salt
½ teaspoon freshly ground black pepper
¼ teaspoon paprika
Chopped parsley, for serving

1. Preheat the oven to 325°F. Grease a 3-quart baking dish with olive oil and set it aside.

2. Bring a large pot of salted water to a boil over high heat. Add the pasta and cook for 1 minute less than the package directions for al dente. Drain the pasta, transfer it back to the pot, and drizzle it with olive oil.

3. Add both cheeses to a large bowl, toss to combine, and then divide into three piles. You'll use 3 cups for the sauce, 1½ cups for the inner layer, and 1½ cups for the topping.

4. In a large saucepan, melt the butter over medium heat. Add the flour and whisk to combine. Cook for 1 minute, whisking. Slowly pour in the milk, whisking constantly, until the sauce is smooth. Slowly pour in the half-and-half and whisk until combined and smooth. Cook, whisking often, until the sauce thickens slightly.

5. Remove the pan from the heat and stir in the salt, pepper, and paprika. Add 1½ cups of the cheeses and stir until melted and smooth. Add another 1½ cups of cheese and stir until melted and smooth.

6. In a large bowl, combine the drained pasta with the cheese sauce, stirring to coat the pasta. Pour half of the pasta mixture into the prepared baking dish. Layer on 1½ cups of the shredded cheese. Add the remaining pasta, smoothing it out with a wooden spoon, and then layer on the remaining 1½ cups of shredded cheese.

7. Bake the casserole for 15 minutes, until the cheese is bubbling and golden brown in places.

8. Remove from the oven and sprinkle with parsley before serving.

SUNDAY FUNDAY STROGANOFF

→→→→→→→→→ ←←←←←←←←←

PAIRED WITH A GLASS OF WINE AND GAMES, this velvety dish is perfect for Muriel's Sunday Funday. Serve it on a bed of egg noodles and follow it with Hope's Strawberry Cream Cheese Pie (page 124) for an unforgettable afternoon with friends.

Serves 4

2 tablespoons olive oil

1 pound top sirloin, boneless ribeye, or beef tenderloin, thinly sliced

2 tablespoons unsalted butter

½ medium onion, finely chopped

8 ounces brown mushrooms, thickly sliced

1 clove garlic, minced

1 tablespoon all-purpose flour

1 cup beef broth

¾ cup heavy whipping cream

¼ cup sour cream

1 tablespoon Worcestershire sauce

½ teaspoon Dijon mustard

½ teaspoon kosher salt

¼ teaspoon freshly ground black pepper

1. In a Dutch oven, heat the oil until shimmering over medium-high heat. Add the beef in a single layer and sear, without stirring, for 1 minute per side just until browned. (You may need to do this in two batches to avoid overcrowding the pan.) Transfer the seared beef to a plate and tent it with foil to keep warm.

2. To the same pan, add the butter, onion, and mushrooms and cook for 6 to 8 minutes or until no liquid remains and the vegetables are lightly brown. Add the garlic and cook until fragrant, about 1 minute. Add the flour and cook, stirring, for 1 minute more.

3. Add the beef broth and stir, scraping the bottom of the pan. Then add the cream. Simmer for 1 to 2 minutes to thicken the sauce.

4. In a small cup, combine 2 or 3 tablespoons of the sauce and the sour cream, then stir the mixture into the sauce.

5. Add the Worcestershire, mustard, salt, and pepper, and stir to combine. Taste the sauce and adjust the seasoning as desired.

6. Add the beef and juices back to the pan and simmer until heated through before serving.

SPEEDY LASAGNA

>>>>>>>>> <<<<<<<<<

AFTER BEING SEPARATED FOR TWENTY YEARS, Hope is understandably hesitant to spend all day in the kitchen for Doc again. This easy-yet-incredible lasagna is the perfect compromise for the curmudgeonly sweethearts. Opting for no-cook lasagna noodles speeds up the process even more.

Serves 12

1 tablespoon olive oil
1 pound ground beef
1 medium onion, diced
1 clove garlic, minced
Kosher salt and freshly ground black pepper
1 (28-ounce) can crushed tomatoes
1 tablespoon Italian seasoning
1 (15-ounce) package whole milk ricotta
3½ cups shredded mozzarella, divided
1 large egg, beaten
9 no-cook lasagna noodles
¼ cup freshly grated Parmesan
2 tablespoons chopped fresh parsley

1. Preheat the oven to 350°F. Coat a 9 × 13-inch baking dish with nonstick spray.

2. In a large skillet over medium-high heat, heat the oil until shimmering. Add the ground beef, onion, and garlic and cook, stirring and crumbling the beef until it browns evenly, 4 to 5 minutes. Season it with salt and pepper. Pour the beef mixture into a colander over a sink to drain the fat, then return the beef to the pan. Add the tomatoes and Italian seasoning and stir to combine.

3. In a medium bowl, add the ricotta, ½ cup of the mozzarella, and the egg. Stir to combine.

4. Spread 1 cup of the tomato mixture on the bottom of the prepared baking dish. Top with 3 lasagna noodles, spread with half of the ricotta mixture, and evenly sprinkle 1 cup of the mozzarella cheese over all. Repeat with a second layer. Top that with the remaining noodles, tomato mixture, and 1 cup of mozzarella cheese. Sprinkle the Parmesan cheese over all.

5. Cover the pan tightly with aluminum foil and bake until the cheese is bubbling and the noodles are tender, 35 to 45 minutes.

6. Remove the foil, turn the oven to broil, and broil until the cheese begins to brown, 2 to 3 minutes more. Remove the lasagna from the oven and let it rest for 10 minutes. Sprinkle it with the parsley before serving.

BIRTHDAY IN A POKE BOWL

→>→>→>→>→> ←←←←←←←←

MEL MAY BE THRILLED WITH PREACHER'S CATFISH AND KALE SALADS, but Jack's surprise of birthday sushi hits the spot. This poke bowl packs all of that LA flavor and more. Just make sure you use sushi-grade fish and you can customize the rest of the bowl however you like it.

Serves 4

2 cups brown rice

¼ cup mayonnaise

1 tablespoon sriracha

2 tablespoons soy sauce

2 tablespoons rice vinegar

2 tablespoons olive oil

1 tablespoon toasted sesame oil

1 tablespoon honey

1 tablespoon freshly squeezed lemon juice

12 ounces sushi-grade raw salmon, thinly sliced

1 avocado, peeled, pitted, and thinly sliced

2 cups salad greens

1 cup shelled edamame

1 cup chopped fresh pineapple

½ cup French fried onions

1 teaspoon sesame seeds

1. Cook the rice according to package directions and keep it warm.

2. Add the mayonnaise and sriracha to a small bowl and whisk to combine. Set aside.

3. In another small bowl, whisk together the soy sauce, vinegar, olive oil, sesame oil, honey, and lemon juice to make the dressing.

4. Divide the warm rice among four large soup or rice bowls. Top each with salmon, avocado slices, salad greens, edamame, pineapple, and fried onions. Sprinkle everything with the sesame seeds and a drizzle of the aioli and dressing.

HELPFUL HOUSEGUEST YAKISOBA

COOKING A MOUTHWATERING MEAL FOR YOUR HOSTS LIKE DENNY DOES IS A GREAT WAY TO REPAY THEIR HOSPITALITY. Of course, paying off Doc's mortgage doesn't hurt either! Luckily, this flavorful Japanese stir-fry tastes like a million bucks.

Serves 4

6 ounces dried yakisoba noodles
1 tablespoon sesame oil
3 tablespoons peanut oil
2 tablespoons minced ginger
2 boneless pork chops, thinly sliced
1 small head Napa or savoy cabbage, shredded (about 4 cups)
2 carrots, peeled and julienned
Kosher salt
2 tablespoons ketchup
¼ cup soy sauce
¼ cup Worcestershire sauce
2 tablespoons mirin or 1 tablespoon sugar
Tabasco sauce, to taste

1. Cook the noodles according to the package directions, then drain them in a colander and run them under cold water. Transfer them to a large bowl, add the sesame oil, and toss to coat.

2. In a large skillet over medium-high heat, heat the peanut oil until shimmering. Stir in the ginger and cook until fragrant, about 1 minute. Add the pork and cook until no pink remains and the edges are golden brown, about 5 minutes.

3. Add the cabbage and carrots, sprinkle with salt, and stir to combine. Cook until the vegetables soften, about 5 minutes. Add a few tablespoons of water if needed to prevent the vegetables from sticking.

4. In a small bowl, add the ketchup, soy sauce, Worcestershire, mirin, and Tabasco to taste and set aside. Stir to combine and cook until the vegetables soften and the liquid has evaporated. Add the noodles and sauce to the skillet and toss to coat everything with the sauce. Continue cooking until the noodles are warmed through.

LOBSTER À LA ARTHUR'S

>>>>>>>>> <<<<<<<<<

WITH THE PORT CITY OF EUREKA NEARBY, slipping away for an evening of incredible seafood and lovely company is a no-brainer. Thankfully, so is making these lobster tails at home. Finish them off with not one but two desserts, Hope McCrea style!

Serves 2

2 (8-ounce) lobster tails

3 tablespoons unsalted butter, melted, plus more for serving

1 teaspoon kosher salt

1 teaspoon freshly ground black pepper

1 teaspoon garlic powder

1 teaspoon paprika

1 teaspoon lemon juice

1 teaspoon chopped fresh parsley

Lemon wedges, for serving

1. Preheat the oven to 450°F. Line a baking sheet with parchment paper.

2. Using kitchen shears, cut the top of the lobster shell straight down the middle toward the fins (don't cut the fins). Use a spoon to separate the meat from the shell, keeping the shell intact. Gently pull open the shell.

3. In a small bowl, combine the butter, salt, pepper, garlic powder, paprika, lemon juice, and parsley, then brush the mixture over the lobster meat.

4. Place the tails on the prepared baking sheet and bake until the lobster is tender and fully cooked, 12 to 15 minutes. Serve with lemon wedges and more melted butter for dipping.

SMOOTH-TALKING CEDAR-PLANK SALMON AND VEGGIES

>>>>>>>>>> <<<<<<<<<<

WITH HONEY, GARLIC, AND LEMON, this gorgeous cedar-plank salmon could even take the edge off of eating with narcissistic sisters-in-law. That's probably why Mel makes it for Mark's sister, Stacy. Just be sure to soak your cedar plank for at least 30 minutes before grilling.

Serves 4

2 (7 × 12-inch) cedar plank boards
4 cloves garlic, minced
1 tablespoon Dijon mustard
2 tablespoons honey
1½ teaspoons chopped fresh rosemary
1 tablespoon chopped fresh thyme
2 tablespoons unsalted butter, melted
Kosher salt and freshly ground black pepper
Four 4-ounce salmon fillets, skin removed
1 large lemon, sliced

1. Soak the cedar planks in water to cover for at least 30 minutes.

2. Preheat half of the grill to medium-high heat, about 400°F.

3. In a small bowl, stir together the garlic, mustard, honey, rosemary, thyme, melted better, and salt and pepper to taste.

4. Place 2 salmon fillets, skin-side down, on each cedar plank. Brush each fillet with the garlic-mustard sauce and top with two slices of lemon.

5. Place the cedar planks on the indirect heat side of the grill and lower the cover. Grill the salmon until the thickest part reaches 135°F and flakes easily with a fork, 20 to 25 minutes.

RELAXING OVEN-BAKED RAINBOW TROUT

→→→→→→→→→→→ ←←←←←←←←←←

WHEN YOU LIVE BY THE RIVER, fishing is as much about letting the sights and sounds (and solitude) soothe your soul as it is about putting something fresh and tasty on the table. That might be why Jack and Doc often come home empty handed after a day by the water. But if you're lucky enough to come by some fresh trout, this quick and easy recipe is the one to reach for.

Serves 4

4 (4-ounce) rainbow trout fillets
3 tablespoons olive oil
2 teaspoons lemon juice
2 cloves garlic, minced
2 teaspoons chopped fresh dill
½ teaspoon paprika
3 teaspoons chopped fresh parsley, divided
¾ teaspoon sea salt
¼ teaspoon freshly ground black pepper
1 large lemon, thinly sliced

1. Preheat the oven to 400°F and line a medium baking sheet or shallow pan with foil or parchment paper.

2. In a small bowl, whisk together the olive oil, lemon juice, garlic, dill, paprika, and 2 tablespoons of the parsley.

3. Move the fish fillets to the prepared pan. Use paper towels to pat them dry, brush both sides with the seasoned olive-oil mixture, then season both sides with salt and pepper. Place the fillets skin-side down in the pan, then top them with the lemon slices.

4. Bake the fillets for 10 to 12 minutes, until the internal temperature reaches 145°F and flakes easily with a fork. Sprinkle with the remaining parsley before serving.

SMALL-TOWN STRAWBERRY JAM

→→→→→→→→→→ ←←←←←←←←←←

NO SMALL TOWN WOULD BE COMPLETE WITHOUT SOMEONE WHO MAKES HOMEMADE STRAWBERRY JAM. The fact that it's Muriel may be a little surprising. But with a recipe this quick and simple, anyone can whip up a scrumptious jar of jam in no time.

Makes one 8-ounce jar

1 pound fresh strawberries, hulled and sliced
1½ cups sugar
2 tablespoons lemon juice
½ teaspoon lemon zest (optional)

1. In a medium saucepan, add the strawberries and sugar and stir well. Bring everything to a boil over medium heat, stirring constantly.

2. When the mixture reaches a boil, add the lemon juice and zest (if using). Continue to boil, stirring to prevent sticking, until the jam reaches 220°F on an instant-read thermometer, about 15 minutes.

3. Pour the finished jam into an 8-ounce jar and allow it to cool.

4. Once the jam is cool, cover it with a lid and store it in the refrigerator for up to 2 weeks.

SUNSHINE STATE FRUIT SMOOTHIE

→→→→→→→→→ ←←←←←←←←←

THERE'S SOMETHING TO BE SAID FOR FRESH AIR AND CALIFORNIA SUNSHINE! Why not combine some healthy habits like Joey does by taking this sweet LA-style smoothie to-go on your next walk? And don't forget your furry friend!

Serves 2

2 cups frozen strawberries
1 banana, fresh or frozen, broken up
1 cup favorite milk
½ cup plain yogurt
2 teaspoons honey (optional)
½ teaspoon chia seeds (optional)

1. Place the strawberries and banana in the blender, then add the milk, yogurt, honey (if using), and chia seeds (if using).

2. Blend until smooth and serve immediately.

EXTRA COZY HOT COCOA

>>>>>>>>>>> <<<<<<<<<<

Whether you whip this hot cocoa up for your little ones like Preacher does for Christopher or you want a warm treat for cozying up by the fire yourself, this cinnamon-infused hot cocoa hits the spot. Top it off with homemade whipped cream or as many marshmallows as you can handle!

Serves 4

4 cups whole milk

¼ cup unsweetened cocoa powder

¼ cup sugar

½ cup bittersweet or semisweet chocolate chips

¼ teaspoon pure vanilla extract

Whipped cream, for serving

Ground cinnamon, for dusting

4 cinnamon sticks, for serving

1. In a small saucepan, add the milk, cocoa powder, and sugar and heat over medium-low heat, whisking, until warm (not boiling). Whisk in the chocolate chips until melted and combined.

2. Remove the cocoa from the heat and whisk in the vanilla.

3. Divide the cocoa among four mugs and top each with a dollop of whipped cream, a dusting of cinnamon, and a cinnamon stick.

PEANUT BUTTER DOG TREATS FOR TUCKER

>>>>>>>>>> <<<<<<<<<

CHARMAINE'S NEED TO NEST CERTAINLY WORKS OUT WELL FOR TUCKER, who's the lucky recipient of some scrumptious-looking homemade treats. This simple recipe makes quick work of whipping them up so you can get back to pampering your pup in other ways. (Just remember to check your peanut butter label for xylitol, which is toxic to dogs.)

Makes 24 dog treats

2½ cups whole wheat flour, rice flour, or coconut flour, plus more for dusting

1 large egg

1 cup natural peanut butter (without xylitol)

1 cup water

2 tablespoons honey

1. Preheat the oven to 350°F. Line two baking sheets with parchment paper.

2. In a large bowl, stir together the flour and egg until combined. Add the peanut butter, water, and honey and stir to make a stiff, sticky dough.

3. Turn out the dough onto a lightly floured surface and roll it into a slab about ½ inch thick. Use a bone-shaped cookie cutter to cut out as many treats as you can. Gather the dough and roll it out again to make more treats.

4. Place the treats on the prepared baking sheets and bake until golden, 18 to 20 minutes.

5. Transfer finished treats to a cooling rack and let them cool completely before moving them to an airtight container to be stored on the counter.

AT THE BAR

The residents of Virgin River don't come to Jack's for the drinks—they come for the food. In Preacher's practiced hands, an ordinary burger becomes a delicious farm-to-table experience. From the spicy duck tacos and freshly caught catfish to the kale salad that makes Mel a believer, it's no wonder everyone craves his cooking. And it doesn't hurt that he serves it all up with a smile that could melt the ice in your lemonade.

TRAVEL-FREE WINGS

→→→→→→→→→ ←←←←←←←←←

TEMPTING AS IT MIGHT BE TO USE THE PROMISE OF WINGS AS A DECOY FOR A SURPRISE CAMPING TRIP, learn from Mel's mistake: skip the puddle jumper and enjoy the wings with your sweetheart instead. These citrusy honey-barbecue baked wings are special enough!

Serves 8

FOR THE SEASONING MIX
1 teaspoon kosher salt
1 teaspoon freshly ground black pepper
1 teaspoon smoked paprika
1 teaspoon garlic powder
½ teaspoon onion powder
¼ teaspoon cayenne pepper

FOR THE ORANGE-HONEY BARBECUE SAUCE
2 teaspoons salted butter
2 teaspoons minced garlic
1 cup barbecue sauce
½ cup honey
¼ cup pulp-free orange juice
2 tablespoons light brown sugar
¼ teaspoon cayenne pepper

2½ pounds chicken wings, disjointed with tips removed
2 teaspoons baking powder
Chopped scallions, for serving

1. Preheat the oven to 425°F. Line a baking sheet with parchment paper.

2. To make the seasoning mix: In a small bowl, stir together the seasonings.

3. To make the barbecue sauce: In a medium pot, melt the butter over medium heat. Add the garlic and cook for 30 seconds. Add the barbecue sauce, honey, juice, sugar, and cayenne and stir to combine. Bring to a simmer, then decrease the heat to low and cook for 10 minutes, stirring.

4. Pat the chicken wings dry with a paper towel, then sprinkle them with the baking powder. Sprinkle with the seasoning mix and toss to coat.

5. Spread the chicken wings on the prepared baking sheet and bake for 20 minutes, then use tongs to turn them over. Bake for 25 minutes longer.

6. Remove the wings from the oven and decrease the temperature to 400°F. Brush the wings liberally with the sauce on both sides, then continue baking them until the glaze is sticky and bubbling, 7 to 8 minutes. Sprinkle with scallions and serve.

ICE-BREAKING ARTICHOKE DIP

→→→→→→→→→→ ←←←←←←←←←←

A MEET-CUTE OVER ARTICHOKES THAT LEADS TO WINE AND CHARCUTERIE? That's reason enough to give Preacher's organic artichoke dip a try. Serve it with crostata or chips for a perfectly enchanting appetizer for two (or ten).

Serves 10

Cooking spray
8 ounces cream cheese, softened
1 cup sour cream
1¼ cups marinated artichoke hearts, coarsely chopped
1 teaspoon minced garlic
½ teaspoon kosher salt
¼ teaspoon freshly ground black pepper
½ cup grated Parmesan cheese
2 tablespoons sliced green onion
1 tablespoon chopped parsley
1½ cups shredded mozzarella cheese, divided

1. Preheat the oven to 375°F. Coat a small baking dish with cooking spray.

2. In a bowl, stir together the cream cheese, sour cream, artichoke hearts, garlic, salt, pepper, Parmesan, green onions, parsley, and ¾ cup of the mozzarella.

3. Spread the mixture in the prepared dish. Sprinkle with the remaining ¾ cup of mozzarella.

4. Bake the dip for 20 minutes or until it is bubbling and the cheese is melted. Set the oven to broil and cook for 2 to 3 minutes or until the cheese starts to brown around the edges.

5. Remove the dip from the oven and serve immediately.

SOOTHING CHICKEN NOODLE SOUP

>>>>>>>>>> <<<<<<<<<

CHARMAINE IS LUCKY TO HAVE SOMEONE AS THOUGHTFUL AS JACK, who knows there's nothing better than homemade chicken noodle soup to soothe the stomach and the soul. If you've never added lemon juice to yours, prepare to be amazed by the way it brings out the soup's flavors!

Serves 6

2 tablespoons unsalted butter
1 medium onion, diced
2 large carrots, peeled and sliced
2 large celery ribs, diced
3 cloves garlic, minced
8 cups chicken stock
2 bay leaves
Kosher salt and freshly ground black pepper
2½ pounds bone-in, skinless chicken breasts
2½ cups wide egg noodles
1 cup frozen peas
2 tablespoons chopped fresh parsley
2 tablespoons chopped fresh dill
1 tablespoon freshly squeezed lemon juice, or more to taste

1. In a large pot or Dutch oven, melt the butter over medium heat. Add the onion, carrots, and celery and cook, stirring occasionally, until the vegetables are tender, 3 to 4 minutes. Add the garlic and cook for about 1 minute more.

2. Add the chicken stock and bay leaves, then season with salt and pepper. Stir to combine. Add the chicken, cover with the lid, and bring it to a boil. Lower the heat and simmer, covered, until the chicken is cooked through, 30 to 40 minutes. Using a slotted spoon, remove the bay leaves and transfer the chicken to a cutting board. Allow it to cool, then chop it into bite-size pieces. Discard the bones and cartilage and return the chicken to the pot.

3. Add the egg noodles and cook until tender, 6 to 7 minutes. Add the peas about 2 minutes before the noodles have finished cooking.

4. Remove the pot from the heat and stir in the parsley, dill, and lemon juice. Taste and adjust the seasonings as needed.

JERK CHICKEN PICK-ME-UP

>>>>>>>>>>> <<<<<<<<<<

WHEN BERT NEEDS A PICK-ME-UP AFTER A LONG, RAINY DAY'S WORK, Jack knows just what to suggest: a jerk chicken that will knock his socks off. This perfectly spiced chicken pairs beautifully with Bert's beverage of choice—an ice-cold beer. If you want a little less heat, make sure you remove the seeds and ribs from the peppers before adding them in.

Serves 8

1 medium onion, coarsely chopped
3 scallions, chopped
2 Scotch bonnet chiles, chopped
2 cloves garlic, minced
1 tablespoon five-spice powder
1 tablespoon ground allspice
1 tablespoon coarsely ground pepper
1 teaspoon dried thyme
1 teaspoon ground nutmeg
1 teaspoon kosher salt
½ cup soy sauce
1 tablespoon vegetable oil
2 (3½- to 4-pound) chickens, quartered
Lime wedges, for serving

1. Add the onion, scallions, chiles, garlic, five-spice powder, allspice, pepper, thyme, nutmeg, and salt to a large food processor and process them into a coarse paste. With the machine running, slowly and steadily pour in the soy sauce and oil.

2. Pour the marinade into a large, shallow dish, and turn the chicken in it to coat. Cover the marinating chicken and refrigerate it overnight.

3. Remove the chicken from the refrigerator and allow it to come to room temperature. Prepare a grill to medium-high heat. Place the chicken on the grates and cover the grill. Cook, turning occasionally, until the skin is deep brown and the meat registers 165°F on an instant-read thermometer, 35 to 40 minutes. Serve with lime wedges.

BRIGHT SIDE BARBECUE CHICKEN SALAD

>>>>>>>>> <<<<<<<<<

STRESS-EATING DOESN'T HAVE TO MEAN HEADING FOR THE NEAREST TUB OF ICE CREAM. (Although, if your house burned down, no one would blame you.) Take a page from Mel's book and opt for this barbecue chicken salad, which tastes like comfort food without the extra calories.

Serves 4

FOR THE DRESSING
¼ cup chopped cilantro
1 tablespoon lime juice
½ teaspoon lime zest
1 tablespoon powdered ranch mix
½ jalapeño pepper, minced (remove seeds for less heat)
1 teaspoon minced garlic
¼ cup mayonnaise
¼ cup buttermilk
Kosher salt and freshly ground black pepper

FOR THE CHICKEN
2½ cups shredded rotisserie chicken
½ cup barbecue sauce, plus more to taste

FOR THE SALAD
8 cups salad greens
1 cup black beans, drained and rinsed
1 cup frozen corn, thawed
1 cup grape tomatoes, halved
¼ cup chopped cilantro
½ cup diced red onion
1 avocado, peeled, pitted, and sliced

1. To make the dressing: Combine all of the dressing ingredients in a blender and blend until smooth. Taste and adjust the seasoning. Transfer to a jar and chill in the refrigerator until ready to serve.

2. To make the chicken: In a medium bowl, add the chicken and pour the barbecue sauce over. Toss to coat evenly. If desired, add more barbecue sauce to taste.

3. To make the salad: Divide the lettuce among four salad bowls or plates. Arrange the beans, corn, tomatoes, cilantro, red onion, and avocado on top. Add a scoop of the chicken and drizzle the dressing over all.

SPECIAL SPICY DUCK TACOS WITH CRANBERRY SALSA

>>>>>>>>>>> <<<<<<<<<<

GOURMET WILD-GAME TACOS LIKE THESE AREN'T YOUR ORDINARY BAR FARE, which is why they make the specials menu at Jack's. Preacher doesn't do ordinary. Adding bright cranberries and spicy jalapeño to duck meat makes these tacos sing.

Serves 3 to 4

2 tablespoons olive oil
1 (7½-ounce) package shredded duck confit meat, pre-cooked

FOR THE CRANBERRY SALSA

1 cup fresh or frozen cranberries
½ medium jalapeño pepper, diced
¼ cup sugar
1 large lime, peeled and juiced, divided
1 tablespoon water
¼ cup apple cider vinegar
½ teaspoon sea salt
¼ teaspoon freshly ground black pepper

FOR THE CABBAGE SLAW

¼ cup olive oil
½ teaspoon ground cumin
½ teaspoon sea salt
1 cup purple cabbage, thinly sliced

FOR SERVING

6–8 corn tortillas

1. Warm the olive oil in a large nonstick pan over medium heat. Stir in the duck meat and cook until hot and lightly browned, about 5 minutes. Remove the pan from the heat and set it aside.

2. To make the cranberry salsa: Combine the cranberries, jalapeño, sugar, lime peel, and water in a small saucepan over low heat. Cook, stirring occasionally, until the sugar has fully dissolved.

3. Stir in the apple cider vinegar, half of the lime juice, salt, and pepper. Increase the heat to medium and cook, stirring occasionally, until the cranberries burst.

4. To make the cabbage slaw: Whisk together the olive oil, remaining lime juice, cumin, and salt in a medium bowl. Add the purple cabbage and toss until well combined. Let this marinate for at least 10 minutes.

5. Warm the tortillas in a medium pan over low heat. Divide the duck meat, cranberry salsa, and cabbage slaw evenly between the tortillas, and serve.

COMFORTING POTATO AND SAUSAGE CASSEROLE

NOTHING COMFORTS LIKE GOOD, homemade food. When Tara suffers a terrible loss, half the town shows up with baked goods and casseroles. But this cheesy dish from Doc is her favorite. With a recipe this simple and delicious, it'll soon be your favorite, too!

Serves 6

Cooking spray
3 large potatoes, peeled and cubed
1 pound skinless smoked sausage, halved and cut into ½-inch pieces
4 tablespoons unsalted butter
4 tablespoons all-purpose flour
2 cups whole milk
8 ounces Cheddar or Monterey Jack cheese, cubed
½ teaspoon kosher salt
¼ teaspoon freshly ground black pepper
⅛ teaspoon paprika
½ cup shredded Cheddar cheese

1. Preheat the oven to 350°F. Grease a 2-quart casserole dish with cooking spray.

2. Bring a large pot of salted water to a boil, add the cubed potatoes, and cook until fork-tender. Drain in a colander.

3. In a large skillet over medium heat, add the sausage and fry, turning occasionally, until browned and cooked through, about 15 minutes. Drain it in a colander.

4. Spread the cooked potatoes and sausage in the prepared casserole dish.

5. In a saucepan, melt the butter over medium heat. Add the flour and cook, stirring constantly, until bubbling and thickened. Slowly pour in the milk and stir until fully combined and starting to thicken slightly. Add the cubed cheese, salt, pepper, and paprika and stir to combine. Cook until the cheese is melted and the sauce is smooth.

6. Pour the sauce over the potatoes and sausage in the casserole dish. Sprinkle with the shredded cheese and bake until the sauce is bubbling and starting to brown around the edges, 35 to 40 minutes. Turn on the broiler and bake for 2 to 3 minutes, until the top is browned in a few places.

STOCK UP ON ELK STEW

→→→→→→→→→→ ←←←←←←←←←←

TAKE A TIP FROM PREACHER AND KEEP A STASH OF THIS SAVORY ELK STEW IN THE FREEZER
AT ALL TIMES—you're going to crave it. Browning the meat brings out its flavor before it
simmers to tender perfection in the pot.

Serves 8

4 tablespoons unsalted butter, divided

2 pounds elk stew meat, such as shoulder
or shank

Kosher salt

½ cup all-purpose flour

1 large yellow onion, chopped

4 cloves garlic, minced

1 ounce dried porcini mushrooms, crushed

2–3 tablespoons canned green chiles,
chopped

4 cups elk, venison, or beef stock

1 pint Belgian beer

2 large carrots, peeled and cut into chunks

1 parsnip, peeled and cut into chunks

1 tablespoon minced fresh sage

1 (15-ounce) can Great Northern beans,
drained and rinsed

1. In a large soup pot, melt 2 tablespoons of the
butter over medium-high heat. Season the
stew meat with salt, then dust it with the
flour. Add the meat to the pot in batches and
brown on all sides, making sure not to
overcrowd the pan. Transfer the meat to a
bowl.

2. Melt the remaining 2 tablespoons of butter
in the pot, add the onion, and cook until
browned, 8 to 10 minutes. Add the garlic and
stir to combine.

3. Return the meat and any juices to the pot.
Add the dried mushrooms, green chiles,
stock, and beer. Bring to a simmer, add salt to
taste, partially cover the pot with a lid, and
cook over medium-low heat for 2 hours.

4. Add the carrots, parsnip, and sage and cook
until the vegetables are tender, about
40 minutes. Add the beans and heat through.
Taste and adjust the seasonings.

A BURGER WORTH WAITING FOR

ALTHOUGH BERT'S GOT PLACES TO BE AND PEOPLE TO TOW, some burgers are just worth waiting for. This one, stuffed with sharp Cheddar and topped with bacon and caramelized onions, is definitely one of those burgers.

Serves 4

8 slices thick-cut bacon
1 sweet yellow onion, sliced
1½ pounds ground beef (80% lean)
1 cup shredded sharp Cheddar cheese
¼ teaspoon kosher salt
¼ teaspoon freshly ground black pepper
1½ teaspoons unsalted butter
Olive oil, for cooking
4 hamburger buns, toasted
Barbecue sauce, for serving

1. In a large skillet, cook the bacon over medium-low heat to your desired doneness. Transfer to a paper towel–lined plate. Drain all but about 1 tablespoon of the grease from the pan.

2. Increase the heat to medium, add the onion, and cook in the reserved bacon grease until golden brown, 8 to 10 minutes. Transfer it to a separate plate.

3. Divide the beef into eight equal portions and shape it into ½-inch-thick patties.

4. Top each patty with ⅛ cup of the Cheddar cheese, 1 or 2 tablespoons of the onions, and another ⅛ cup of cheese, leaving a bare edge around the patty. Top with another patty and press the edges together to create a seal, making sure there are no places where the cheese can leak out. Season with salt and pepper.

5. In the same skillet, melt the butter over medium heat. Add a drizzle of olive oil and stir to combine. Working in batches, add the burgers and cook until brown on one side, about 8 minutes. Using a wide spatula, carefully flip the burgers and continue cooking until golden brown on that side, about 5 minutes.

6. Open the burger buns, spread barbecue sauce on each side, and top each with a burger, two bacon strips, and any remaining onions.

BETTER THAN YOUR USUAL MEATLOAF

>>>>>>>>>> <<<<<<<<<

WITH A FULL BAR AND JACK AND PREACHER BOTH OFF-SITE, skipping the specials board is a smart move on Ricky's part. But who needs specials when you have meatloaf this good? The secret is in the sauce.

Serves 8

FOR THE MEATLOAF
2 pounds ground beef (85% lean)
1 medium onion, finely chopped
2 large eggs
3 cloves garlic, minced
3 tablespoons ketchup
3 tablespoons finely chopped fresh parsley
¾ cup panko breadcrumbs
⅓ cup 2% milk
1½ teaspoons kosher salt
1½ teaspoons Italian seasoning
¼ teaspoon freshly ground black pepper
½ teaspoon paprika

FOR THE SAUCE
¾ cup ketchup
1½ teaspoons white vinegar
2½ tablespoons brown sugar
1 teaspoon garlic powder
½ teaspoon onion powder
¼ teaspoon freshly ground black pepper
¼ teaspoon kosher salt

1. Preheat the oven to 375°F. Line a 9 × 5-inch loaf pan with parchment paper.

2. To make the meatloaf: In a large bowl, add all of the ingredients and mix with clean hands to fully combine. Be gentle so as not to compact the meat.

3. Gently press the meat into the prepared pan, shape the top, and bake for 40 minutes.

4. To make the sauce: In a small bowl, stir all the ingredients together. Spread the sauce over the meatloaf, then continue baking until the temperature registers 160°F on an instant-read thermometer, 15 to 20 minutes.

5. Remove from the oven, brush the top with more sauce, and let the meatloaf rest for 10 minutes before slicing. Drizzle with any juices from the pan and any remaining sauce.

ONE TRICK STEAK

Jack seems to know how to cook just one thing: steak. But if this chimichurri-topped steak is the only main dish you know how to make, you'll still be ahead in the kitchen. Serve it medium-rare with a vodka martini (or whatever beverage is handy).

Serves 4

FOR THE CHIMICHURRI SAUCE

1 small shallot, minced

1 red jalapeño pepper, seeded and minced (optional)

4 cloves garlic, minced

½ cup apple cider vinegar

1 teaspoon kosher salt

¼ cup finely chopped fresh cilantro

¼ cup finely chopped fresh parsley

¼ cup finely chopped fresh kale

2 tablespoons finely chopped fresh oregano

¾ cup extra-virgin olive oil

FOR THE STEAK

2 pounds tri-tip steak

Kosher salt and freshly ground black pepper

2 tablespoons unsalted butter

2 tablespoons olive oil

1. To make the chimichurri: In a medium bowl, combine the shallot, jalapeño, garlic, vinegar, and salt. Let marinate for 10 minutes. Add the cilantro, parsley, kale, oregano, and oil and stir to combine. Set this aside.

2. To make the steak: Let the steak come to room temperature before cooking. Season it on both sides with salt and pepper.

3. In a large cast-iron skillet, heat the butter and oil over medium-high heat. Add the steak and sear it on each side for 4 to 5 minutes, then cook until your desired doneness: 125°F for rare, 130°F for medium-rare, 135°F for medium.

4. Slice the steak against the grain and serve it topped with the chimichurri sauce.

SEMPER FI SPAGHETTI AND MEATBALLS

THIS IS THE KIND OF DISH THAT FILLS YOU UP SO YOU CAN IMPROVISE, adapt, and overcome—even if you're just heading out on the trails for the day like Jack and his Marine buddies. And you can adapt this satisfying recipe by using whatever pasta you happen to have on hand.

Serves 6 to 8

FOR THE MEATBALLS

3 slices white bread, crusts removed, torn into pieces
⅔ cup cold water
1 pound lean ground beef (85% or 90% lean)
1 pound sweet Italian sausage, casings removed
¼ cup grated Parmesan cheese, plus more for serving
4 cloves garlic, minced
1 teaspoon kosher salt
½ teaspoon freshly ground black pepper
1 large egg
¾ cup all-purpose flour
3 tablespoons vegetable oil

FOR THE SAUCE

3 tablespoons olive oil (optional)
1 medium yellow onion, chopped
4 cloves garlic, minced
1 (28-ounce) can crushed tomatoes
1 pint cherry tomatoes
2 bay leaves (optional)
Kosher salt and freshly ground black pepper
2 tablespoons minced fresh basil, plus more for serving

1 pound spaghetti
Fresh basil, for serving

1. To make the meatballs: In a bowl, combine the bread and water and set it aside for 5 minutes, then mash it with a fork.

2. In a large bowl, add the beef, sausage, Parmesan, garlic, salt, black pepper, egg, and mashed bread. Using clean hands, mix gently until combined. Form the mixture into 1½-inch meatballs. Spread the flour on a plate and lightly dredge the meatballs, dusting off any excess.

3. In a heavy skillet, heat the oil over medium heat. Add the meatballs in two batches and cook them without overcrowding the pan until browned on all sides, about 6 minutes. Remove from the pan and set aside.

4. To make the sauce: In the same skillet, heat the olive oil (if needed) over medium heat until shimmering. Add the onion and cook, stirring often, until soft and golden brown, about 5 minutes. Add the garlic and cook for 1 minute.

5. Add the crushed tomatoes, cherry tomatoes, and bay leaves (if using) and stir to combine. Bring everything to a simmer.

6. Add the meatballs to the sauce, partially cover with a lid, and gently simmer for 30 minutes, turning the meatballs occasionally, until the cherry tomatoes have burst and the meatballs are cooked through. Remove the bay leaves, stir in the basil, and season with salt and pepper.

7. Meanwhile, in a large pot of salted water, cook the pasta to the desired doneness according to package instructions.

8. Divide the pasta among bowls and ladle the sauce and meatballs on top. Garnish with fresh basil.

HUNTING PARTY HALIBUT

If Preacher is serving this fresh-caught halibut to his big hunting party alongside Dungeness crab, Kobe beef, and Château de Beaucastel wine, you know it's good. Searing it with spices takes the white fish to a new level.

Serves 4

FOR THE DRY RUB
1 teaspoon kosher salt
2 tablespoons paprika
1 tablespoon dried thyme
1 tablespoon dried oregano
1 tablespoon onion powder
1 tablespoon garlic powder
⅛ teaspoon cayenne pepper

Four 6-ounce halibut fillets, skin-on,
    1–1½ inches thick
4 tablespoons unsalted butter
Lemon wedges, for serving

1. To make the dry rub: In a shallow dish, whisk together the rub ingredients.

2. Sprinkle the halibut fillets with the dry rub, pressing it in to help it stick.

3. In a large nonstick skillet, melt the butter over medium-high heat until foaming.

4. Add the fillets, skin-side down, and cook until blackened, 3 to 4 minutes.

5. Flip the fillets over, decrease the heat to medium, and cook until the fish is opaque, about 3 minutes more. Serve the fillets with lemon wedges and the pan juices spooned over the top.

EXTRA-CHEESY TUNA MELT

→→→→→→→→→ ←←←←←←←←←

GOSSIP IS HUNGRY WORK, so it's no wonder Connie's lunch of choice is a protein-packed tuna melt. This one is filled with flavor and extra cheesy, just how she likes it. Feel free to swap the white Cheddar for Swiss, Havarti, provolone, or muenster. You can even mix and match!

Serves 4

1 scallion, thinly sliced

3 tablespoons chopped fresh flat-leaf parsley

2 tablespoons chopped fresh tarragon

Zest of 1 lemon

2 teaspoons lemon juice

1 teaspoon Dijon mustard

⅛ teaspoon freshly ground black pepper

⅓ cup mayonnaise

2 (6-ounce) cans solid white tuna, well drained and flaked

8 slices French or Italian loaf bread

1 large tomato, thinly sliced

4 ounces sharp white Cheddar cheese, grated

2 tablespoons unsalted butter, softened and divided

1. In a medium bowl, combine the scallion, parsley, tarragon, lemon zest, lemon juice, mustard, black pepper, and mayonnaise. Add the drained tuna and mix well, breaking up any large chunks.

2. Divide the tuna mixture evenly among four slices of bread. Top with the tomato slices and one-fourth of the grated cheese. Spread 1 tablespoon of the butter on the remaining four bread slices and place them buttered-side up on top of the cheese.

3. Heat a large cast-iron skillet over medium heat. Place the sandwiches, buttered-side down, in the pan. (You may need to work in batches to avoid overcrowding the pan.) Spread the remaining butter on the top bread slices. Let the sandwiches cook for about 3 minutes, or until golden brown on the bottom.

4. Flip the sandwiches over and cook for 3 minutes more, until the second side is browned and the cheese has melted.

GRILLED CATFISH WORTH RETURNING FOR

MEL MIGHT LONG FOR SOME SUSHI WHEN SHE'S IN VIRGIN RIVER, but the little riverside town has its own perks—like Preacher's grilled catfish. This recipe is so good it'll make you forget all about the city and embrace the simple life. If cilantro (like city life) isn't for you, swap it out for parsley.

Serves 2

FOR THE CILANTRO-LIME BUTTER
2 tablespoons salted butter, softened
1 clove garlic, minced
Juice of ½ large lime
1 tablespoon chopped fresh cilantro

FOR THE BLACKENED SEASONING
1½ tablespoons paprika
1 tablespoon garlic powder
1 tablespoon onion powder
1 tablespoon ground dried thyme
1 teaspoon freshly ground black pepper
1 teaspoon cayenne pepper
1 teaspoon dried basil

2 (6- to 8-ounce) catfish filets
4 teaspoons Blackened Seasoning
Olive oil
Chopped fresh cilantro, for serving
Lime wedges, for serving

1. To make the cilantro-lime butter: Combine the softened butter, garlic, lime juice, and 1 tablespoon of cilantro in a small bowl. (For a deeper flavor, roast the garlic first.) Move the butter to the refrigerator.

2. To make the blackened seasoning: Combine all seasoning ingredients in a small bowl.

3. Preheat a clean grill to medium-high heat. Season both sides of the catfish fillets with blackened seasoning.

4. Lightly brush the grill with olive oil. Place the fillets on the grill and let them cook for 5 to 7 minutes per side until their internal temperature reaches 145°F and the fish flakes easily with a fork.

5. Serve the grilled fillets with a pat of cilantro-lime butter, a bit of fresh cilantro, and a wedge of lime.

KEEPING IT FRESH
COCONUT CURRY SOUP

>>>>>>>>>>> <<<<<<<<<

One of the great things about a small town is being able to walk in and order "the usual." But befriending someone like Preacher, who knows your tastes and can offer up something new and intriguing like this curry soup, is even better. You know you best, though, so remember to adjust the spice level to your taste.

Serves 4

2 tablespoons olive oil
1 medium onion, finely chopped
2 cloves garlic, finely chopped
2½-inch piece ginger, peeled and finely grated
1 tablespoon medium curry powder
¼ teaspoon crushed red pepper flakes
¾ cup red lentils
1 (14.5-ounce) can crushed tomatoes
2½ cups water
½ cup chopped cilantro, plus more for serving
Kosher salt and freshly ground black pepper
1 (13.5-ounce) can unsweetened coconut milk, well shaken, divided
Sliced jalapeños, for serving (optional)
Lime wedges, for serving

1. In a medium saucepan, heat the oil over medium heat until shimmering. Add the onion and cook, stirring often, until softened and golden brown, 8 to 10 minutes.

2. Stir in the garlic, ginger, curry powder, and red pepper flakes until fragrant, about 2 minutes. Add the lentils and cook for 1 minute, stirring to coat with the oil and spices.

3. Add the tomatoes, water, cilantro, and a large pinch of salt, and season with pepper.

4. Reserve ¼ cup of the coconut milk for serving and add the rest to the pot. Bring everything to a boil, then lower the heat to a simmer and cook, stirring often, until the lentils are tender but still hold their shape, about 20 minutes. Taste and adjust the seasonings, if needed.

5. Divide the soup among four bowls. Top each with jalapeño slices, a drizzle of the reserved coconut milk, and a sprinkle of cilantro before serving with lime wedges.

A SURPRISINGLY GOOD HARVEST SALAD

→→→→→→→→→→ ←←←←←←←←←

FINDING A GOURMET SALAD AT A RUSTIC BAR IN THE MIDDLE OF NOWHERE MIGHT JUST BE WHAT TIPS THE SCALES IN VIRGIN RIVER'S FAVOR FOR MEL. With figs, roasted sweet potatoes, and feta warming it up, this incredible autumn-harvest salad will be just as pleasant a surprise for your tastebuds. Make sure your mix includes kale for a full salute to Preacher.

Serves 4

FOR THE ROASTED VEGETABLES
2 large sweet potatoes, peeled and cubed
1 pound Brussels sprouts, halved
2 tablespoons olive oil
½ teaspoon kosher salt
¼ teaspoon freshly ground black pepper

FOR THE DRESSING
1 tablespoon minced shallot
2 tablespoons Dijon mustard
¼ cup freshly squeezed lemon juice
1½ teaspoons lemon zest
2 teaspoons honey or agave nectar
¼ cup olive oil

FOR THE SALAD
4 cups mixed greens
½ cup cooked quinoa
½ cup feta cheese, crumbled
½ cup pomegranate arils
4 large fresh figs, quartered

1. Preheat the oven to 375°F. Line a baking sheet or two with parchment paper.

2. To make the roasted vegetables: Add the sweet potatoes and Brussels sprouts to a large bowl. Drizzle them with the olive oil, season with the salt and pepper, and toss to coat evenly. Spread the vegetables on the prepared baking sheet and roast for 35 to 40 minutes, until golden brown and tender. Remove the pan from the oven and set it aside to cool.

3. To make the dressing: In a jar with a lid, add all of the ingredients and shake to combine.

4. To make the salad: Divide the greens among four serving bowls. Divide the roasted vegetables among the bowls, then top each with an even amount of the quinoa, feta, pomegranate arils, and figs. Finish the salads with a healthy drizzle of the dressing.

SQUIRREL-FREE SQUASH AND LENTILS BOWL

→→→→→→→→→ ←←←←←←←←←

Jack has Mel going for a second when he tells her the lovely vegetarian meal in front of her involves small game. But just like this heartening recipe, her bowl is filled with squash, lentils, and everything she needs to fortify her for her first night in the cabin. (Except for the whiskey.)

Serves 6

2 to 3 tablespoons coconut oil or olive oil
1 medium white onion, diced
3 cloves garlic, minced
1 large rib celery, chopped
2 tablespoons curry powder
1 teaspoon ground cumin
1 cup uncooked red lentils
12 ounces cubed butternut squash
1 cup light or full-fat coconut milk
1 (28-ounce) can diced tomatoes
4 cups vegetable broth
Toasted pepitas, for serving
Cooked chestnuts or toasted walnuts, chopped, for serving
Chopped parsley, for serving

1. In a large soup pot, heat the oil over medium-high heat until shimmering. Add the onion, garlic, and celery and cook until softened and golden, 7 to 8 minutes.

2. Sprinkle the curry powder and cumin over the vegetables and stir to coat; cook for 2 to 3 more minutes.

3. Add the lentils, squash, coconut milk, diced tomatoes, and broth and bring everything to a simmer. Cook, uncovered, until the butternut squash and lentils are tender when pierced with a fork, about 20 minutes.

4. Using an immersion blender, or carefully transferring the soup to a blender in batches, puree the soup to a smooth consistency. Or for a heartier consistency, transfer only 2 cups of the soup to a blender, puree, and pour it back into the pot.

5. Ladle the soup into bowls and garnish with the pepitas, chestnuts, and parsley.

UNCOMPROMISING VEGGIE QUICHE

>>>>>>>>>>> <<<<<<<<<<<

As PREACHER PROVES TIME AND AGAIN, healthy food can be just as incredible as cholesterol-raising fare. Hope might even agree if she bothers to taste the incredible quiche he makes for her. She's right, though: this fluffy vegan dish is no bacon and eggs with cheesy potatoes—it's better!

Serves 6

Cooking spray
1 (14.1-ounce) package pie crusts
1 (14-ounce) block silken tofu
4 tablespoons chickpea flour
2–3 cloves garlic, minced
1 tablespoon nutritional yeast
1½ tablespoons apple cider vinegar
1 tablespoon Dijon mustard
½ teaspoon ground turmeric (optional)
Black salt and freshly ground black pepper
1 large zucchini, sliced into rounds
1 large yellow squash, sliced into rounds
3 large Roma tomatoes, sliced into rounds
½ large bell pepper, chopped
1 teaspoon chopped fresh thyme
1 teaspoon chopped fresh rosemary
1 teaspoon chopped fresh oregano
1 tablespoon chopped fresh parsley

1. Preheat the oven to 350°F. Lightly grease a 9-inch pie pan.

2. Fit one pie crust into the prepared pan and prick the crust all over with a fork to prevent air pockets. (Save the other crust for another recipe.) Move the crust to the refrigerator.

3. Add the silken tofu, chickpea flour, garlic, nutritional yeast, vinegar, mustard, and turmeric, salt, and pepper to a blender and blend until completely smooth.

4. In the pie crust, layer the zucchini, yellow squash, tomatoes, and bell pepper, reserving some to make a pattern on top. Sprinkle the herbs in between the layers and on top.

5. Pour the tofu mixture over the veggies, prodding with a fork to make sure the mixture flows between the vegetables. Decorate the top with the reserved vegetables.

6. Place the pie pan on a baking sheet to catch any overflow and bake until the center is firm when tested with a knife and the crust and top are golden, about 40 minutes. Let the quiche cool for 10 minutes before serving.

FOCACCIA FOR A MIDDAY SURPRISE

→→→→→→→→→ ←←←←←←←←←

Jack never does anything by halves, and his sweet midday surprise of a chicken-focaccia sandwich for Mel is no exception. Infused with garlic and rosemary, this homemade bread makes the perfect base for any sandwich as well as a scrumptious snack all by itself.

Makes 8 large pieces

- 4 cups all-purpose flour or bread flour
- 2 teaspoons kosher salt
- 2 teaspoons instant yeast
- 2 cups lukewarm water
- 4 tablespoons olive oil, divided, plus more for brushing
- 1–2 teaspoons whole rosemary leaves
- 3 cloves garlic, thinly sliced
- Flaky sea salt

1. In a large bowl, whisk together the flour, salt, and yeast. Mix in the water using a silicone spatula until a sticky dough forms, then roll it into a ball. Brush the entire surface of the dough with olive oil. Cover the bowl with plastic wrap and chill in the refrigerator for at least 12 hours or up to 3 days.

2. Line a 9 × 13-inch baking sheet with parchment paper or coat it with nonstick cooking spray. Pour 2 tablespoons of oil onto the parchment and brush it all over.

3. Remove the dough from the refrigerator and use two forks to deflate it and pull it away from the sides. Rotate the bowl as you deflate, gathering the dough into a rough ball. Roll the dough ball in the oil on the pan to coat and press it out into a rough rectangle. Let the dough rest at room temperature for 3 to 4 hours.

4. Place a rack in the middle of the oven and preheat the oven to 425°F.

5. Sprinkle the rosemary over the dough. Pour the remaining 2 tablespoons of oil over the dough, dip your fingers in the oil to coat, and press straight down to create deep dimples, gently stretching the dough to fill the pan. Add the garlic slices, placing some in the dimples. Sprinkle the dough with flaky sea salt.

6. Bake the focaccia for 25 to 30 minutes, until the bottom is golden brown and crisp. Then transfer it to a cooling rack to cool for 10 minutes before slicing and serving.

NO CAMPFIRE REQUIRED S'MORES BARS

As CHRISTOPHER DISCOVERS, s'mores are a pretty good consolation prize for missing out on a sleepover. But turning them into bars makes them a spectacular treat you can pack up and share at the next get-together.

Makes 12 bars

Cooking spray
½ cup unsalted butter
1 large egg
1 cup packed light brown sugar
1 tablespoon vanilla extract
¾ cup all-purpose flour
5 full-size graham crackers, crumbled
1 cup mini marshmallows
1 cup semisweet chocolate chips

1. Preheat the oven to 350°F. Line an 8 × 8-inch baking pan with aluminum foil, coat it with cooking spray, and set it aside.

2. Melt the butter in a large, microwave-safe bowl, then let it cool to room temperature.

3. Stir in the egg, brown sugar, and vanilla to combine. Then add the flour and stir just until combined, being sure not to overmix.

4. Fold in the graham crackers and any crumbs, the marshmallows, and the chocolate chips. Scrape the batter into the prepared pan and smooth out the top.

5. Bake until the center is firm and the edges are set, 20 to 22 minutes. Let the bars cool in the pan for at least 30 minutes before slicing and serving.

IRRESISTIBLE PANNA COTTA

TAKE YOUR CUE FROM MURIEL AND ELEVATE YOUR AFTERNOON PICK-ME-UP. This creamy vanilla-bean panna cotta (based on Preacher's) is as easy to make as it is heavenly to eat. Top it off with fresh berries or sliced fruit for an irresistible treat.

Serves 6

2 cups heavy cream
½ cup sugar
1½ teaspoons vanilla paste or extract
1½ teaspoons unflavored gelatin
½ cup whole milk
½ cup whole-milk Greek yogurt, at room temperature
Sliced strawberries, for serving (optional)

1. In a saucepan, add the cream and sugar and bring them to a simmer over medium-low heat, stirring occasionally. Remove the pan from the heat and add the vanilla, stirring to combine. Let cool.

2. Pour the milk into a small bowl, sprinkle the gelatin over, and let that stand until the gelatin completely softens, about 10 minutes. Stir the gelatin mixture into the cream mixture until dissolved, then stir in the room-temperature yogurt. Strain the mixture into another bowl and set it in an ice bath in the refrigerator to chill.

3. Divide the chilled mixture among six 4-ounce ramekins, cover with plastic wrap and refrigerate until set, at least 6 hours or overnight.

4. Dip the bottom of each ramekin into warm water to loosen the panna cotta and invert it onto a plate. Finish it with a few strawberry slices, if desired.

THIRST-QUENCHING TRIPLE-CITRUS LEMONADE

CHARMAINE MIGHT JUST BE TRYING TO GET RID OF MEL WHEN SHE SENDS HER TO THE BAR FOR PREACHER'S TRIPLE-CITRUS LEMONADE, but this bright beverage is worth a trip. Just don't spill it—you won't want to waste a drop. (And if you're dealing with a particularly difficult patient, you can always add a little rum or vodka to your glass.)

Serves 6

½ cup sugar

½ cup hot water

2 cups cold water

1 cup freshly squeezed and strained orange juice

¼ cup freshly squeezed and strained lime juice

¼ cup freshly squeezed and strained lemon juice

Orange, lime, and lemon slices, for serving

Fresh mint, for serving

1. In a heatproof bowl, stir together the sugar and hot water until the sugar dissolves. Then stir in the cold water and fruit juices.

2. Transfer the lemonade to a pitcher filled with ice and stir in several fruit slices before serving. Store the lemonade in the refrigerator for up to 3 days and serve garnished with a sprig of fresh mint.

SPILL THE SWEET TEA

This sweet iced tea is the perfect companion for midday venting, when it's too early for whiskey. Pour yourself a glass, sip, and process whatever drama is going on in your life, like a surprise visit from your soon-to-be-divorced older sister. You can even infuse the simple syrup with fresh herbs or fruit to take your tea up a notch.

Serves 8

FOR THE SIMPLE SYRUP
1 cup sugar
1 cup water

FOR THE TEA
12 regular-size tea bags
⅛ teaspoon baking soda
4 cups water
4 cups ice cubes, plus more for serving
1–1¼ cups simple syrup

1. To make the simple syrup: In a small saucepan, add the sugar and water over medium-high heat. Bring to a boil, stirring constantly, and cook until the sugar dissolves. Remove it from the heat and let it cool. Store the syrup in an airtight container in the refrigerator for up to 2 weeks.

2. To make the tea: Place the tea bags and baking soda in a large heatproof glass pitcher. In a kettle, bring the water to a boil, then immediately pour it over the tea bags, making sure the bags are covered. Let this steep for 7 minutes.

3. Remove the tea bags without squeezing them. Add the ice and stir until it melts. Stir in the simple syrup, taste, and adjust the sweetness as necessary. Fill eight glasses with ice and pour the tea over top.

THE CLASSIC COSMO

Mel might not have any Cointreau handy that first night in town, but Jack seems like the type to keep it on hand for her after their meet-cute. When you're craving the perfect Cosmopolitan, this classic recipe is the one to reach for.

Serves 1

1 ounce Cointreau
2 ounces vodka
1 ounce cranberry juice
1 ounce freshly squeezed lime juice
Ice
1 orange twist

1. In a cocktail shaker, add the Cointreau, vodka, cranberry juice, and lime juice. Add ice and shake until chilled.

2. Strain the liquid into a chilled cocktail glass and garnish with an orange twist.

YE OLDE MULLED WINE

No Renaissance faire would be complete without a well-stocked tavern serving ale and mulled wine. Luckily, this age-old tipple is just as delicious and simple to make today (with a few modern modifications). For a touch less bitterness, be sure to peel your oranges.

Serves 4 to 6

1 (750-millileter) bottle dry red wine
¼ cup brandy
1 orange, sliced into rounds
8 whole cloves
2 cinnamon sticks
2 star anise
2–4 tablespoons sugar, honey, or maple syrup

1. In a large saucepan, add the wine, brandy, orange slices, cloves, cinnamon, star anise, and 2 tablespoons of the sugar over medium-high heat and stir to combine.

2. Cook until the liquid just begins to simmer (do not let it bubble). Decrease the heat to low, cover, and simmer for at least 15 minutes or up to 3 hours.

3. Strain the mixture into a bowl over a fine-mesh strainer to remove the orange slices, cloves, cinnamon sticks, and star anise. Taste and adjust the sweetness as desired before serving warm in heatproof mugs.

FROM THE
BAKERY TRUCK

Whether it's Paige or Connie at the helm, you can't help but
be captivated by the many marvelous treats coming out of
the bakery truck. Even Lizzie creates a few favorites, once she
gives small-town living (and a certain sweet, military-bound
busboy) a chance. From danishes, scones, and muffins to
cookies, cupcakes, and—of course—a bountiful supply of freshly
baked pies, these ladies know how to satisfy a sweet tooth!

PUT A DANISH
IN YOUR MOUTH

>>>>>>>>> <<<<<<<<<

NOTHING SAYS "I'M SORRY FOR PUTTING MY FOOT IN MY MOUTH" LIKE A SCRUMPTIOUS DANISH, so it's lucky for Paige that she has so many on hand when she implies Doc goes fishing to avoid Hope. Raspberry is a delightful companion to cream cheese, but you can use any jam you like for this recipe.

Makes 18 Danish

FOR THE DANISHES
1 (17.3-ounce) package frozen puff pastry, thawed
1 cup cream cheese, softened
½ cup granulated sugar
2 teaspoons vanilla extract
¾ cup seedless raspberry jam
1 large egg
1 tablespoon water

FOR THE GLAZE
½ cup confectioners' sugar
1–2 tablespoons 2% milk

1. Preheat the oven to 400°F. Line a large baking sheet with parchment paper.

2. To make the Danishes: Line your counter or a flat surface with parchment paper or sprinkle with flour. Lay out the puff pastry sheets on the parchment. Use a 3-inch cookie cutter or glass to cut nine circles from each sheet. Place each circle on the prepared baking sheet. Use a butter knife to lightly score around the edges of each circle to create a border that will hold the filling.

3. In a medium bowl, beat the cream cheese, granulated sugar, and vanilla until light and fluffy. Place a heaping tablespoon of the mixture in the center of each circle. Gently spread out with the back of a spoon and make a depression in the center to hold the jam. Spoon about 2 teaspoons of jam on top of the cream cheese.

4. In a small bowl, whisk the egg and water together, then brush on the edges of each pastry. Bake for 15 to 18 minutes, until the pastry is golden and the jam is bubbling.

5. To make the glaze: In a small bowl, whisk together the confectioners' sugar and milk.

6. Remove the pastries from the oven and transfer to a wire rack to cool. Place a piece of parchment under the rack to catch any drips from the glaze. Drizzle the pastry with the glaze and let it harden before serving.

GOOD MOOD SCONES

WHAT MAKES A GOOD MOOD EVEN BETTER? A fruit-filled scone, especially when it's paired with telling your closest friends you shredded your divorce papers after a surprise proposal. Hope practically dances up to the counter for one of these brightly flavored baked goods.

Makes 8 large scones

FOR THE SCONES
2 cups all-purpose flour, plus more for rolling

½ cup granulated sugar, plus more for sprinkling

2½ teaspoons baking powder

½ teaspoon kosher salt

2 teaspoons orange zest

½ cup unsalted butter, frozen

½ cup heavy cream, plus more for brushing

1 large egg

1 teaspoon vanilla extract

1 heaping cup cranberries, fresh or frozen

FOR THE ORANGE GLAZE
1 cup confectioners' sugar

2–3 tablespoons orange juice

1. To make the scones: In a large bowl, whisk together the flour, granulated sugar, baking powder, salt, and orange zest. Using a box grater, grate the frozen butter over the flour mixture and use a pastry cutter or two forks to work it into pea-size crumbs. Place the mixture in the freezer for 10 minutes.

2. In a small bowl, whisk together the cream, egg, and vanilla. Pour it over the flour mixture, add the cranberries, and stir just until combined. Turn the dough out onto a lightly floured surface and gather it into a ball. The dough will be sticky. Press it into an 8-inch disk and cut it into eight wedges using a sharp knife.

3. Brush the scones with the cream and sprinkle them with granulated sugar. Refrigerate the scones for 15 minutes. Meanwhile, preheat the oven to 400°F. Line a large baking sheet with parchment paper.

4. Place the scones 2 inches apart on the prepared baking sheet. Bake for 22 to 25 minutes or until golden brown. Remove them from the oven, transfer them to a cooling rack, and let them cool.

5. To make the glaze: In a small bowl, whisk together the confectioners' sugar and orange juice. Place a piece of parchment under the rack to catch any drips from the glaze and drizzle it over the scones. Let the glaze harden before serving.

APOLOGY BEAR CLAWS

>>>>>>>>> <<<<<<<<<

HOPE MAY MISS THE EGG RACE, but she's there for Doc through thick and thin. And as she well knows, the best apologies come with coffee and a sweet treat. Iced and almond-infused bear claws like these are just the thing.

Makes 18 bear claws

FOR THE BEAR CLAWS
1 (17.3-ounce) package frozen puff pastry, thawed
1 large egg yolk
1 tablespoon 2% milk
1½ teaspoons honey
1 teaspoon almond extract
3 tablespoons granulated sugar
½ teaspoon ground cinnamon
¾ cup sliced almonds

FOR THE GLAZE
1 cup confectioners' sugar
4 teaspoons 2% milk

1. Preheat the oven to 400°F. Line two baking sheets with parchment paper.

2. Roll out the puff pastry and use a pizza cutter to cut each sheet into nine squares. Fold one side over to make a triangle and press the edges together to seal. Cut six ¾-inch slices evenly along the long edge of each triangle. Cut a 1-inch slit through the point of the triangle on the other side. Fan out the "fingers" and separate the base of the paw to resemble the photo. Place on the prepared baking sheets.

3. In a small bowl, whisk together the egg yolk, milk, honey, and almond extract. Brush this on the top of the bear claws.

4. In another small bowl, add the granulated sugar and ground cinnamon and stir to combine. Sprinkle this evenly over the bear claws, then sprinkle the almonds evenly over all.

5. Bake the bear claws for 14 to 16 minutes, until golden brown. Let them cool on the pans for at least 15 minutes, then transfer them to a wire rack.

6. To make the glaze: In a small bowl, add the confectioners' sugar and milk and whisk until smooth.

7. Place a piece of parchment under the rack to catch any drips from the glaze. Drizzle the bear claws with the glaze and let it harden before serving.

BREATHE DEEPLY AND EAT BLUEBERRY MUFFINS

→→→→→→→→→→ ←←←←←←←←←←

In Virgin River, you never visit a friend empty handed. Doc's sage advice about grief may help Tara more than the muffins he brings her, but muffins never hurt—especially when they're this tasty!

Makes 12 muffins

½ cup unsalted butter, softened
1¼ cups plus 1 tablespoon sugar, divided
2 large eggs
1 teaspoon vanilla extract
2 cups all-purpose flour
½ teaspoon kosher salt
2 teaspoons baking powder
½ cup 2% milk
2 cups fresh blueberries

1. Preheat the oven to 375°F. Fit a muffin tin with paper liners.

2. In a medium bowl with an electric mixer, cream the butter and 1¼ cups of the sugar until light and fluffy. Add and beat the eggs one at a time. Add the vanilla and beat to combine.

3. In a large bowl, sift together the flour, salt, and baking powder. Add half the mixture to the creamed butter mixture and beat to combine. Add half of the milk and beat again. Repeat with the remaining flour and milk, beating well after each addition. Fold in the berries, being careful not to break them.

4. Divide the batter among the muffin cups. Sprinkle the remaining 1 tablespoon of sugar over the tops.

5. Bake for 30 to 35 minutes, or until golden on top and a muffin springs back when lightly touched with a fingertip. Let the muffins cool in the pan for 5 minutes, then transfer to a cooling rack and let cool for 20 more minutes.

PACKABLE PEANUT BUTTER BANANA BREAD

>>>>>>>>> <<<<<<<<<

WHETHER YOU'RE GOING ON AN ADVENTURE LIKE DENNY AND LIZZIE OR YOU'RE JUST HEADED TO WORK, this protein-packed breakfast bread is the perfect fuel. If you're feeling especially audacious, throw a handful of chocolate chips into the batter.

Makes 1 loaf

Cooking spray
1½ cups all-purpose flour
1 teaspoon baking soda
½ teaspoon kosher salt
3 large very ripe bananas, mashed
½ cup creamy peanut butter
4 tablespoons unsalted butter, melted and slightly cooled
¾ cup packed light brown sugar
1 large egg, at room temperature
1 teaspoon vanilla extract

1. Preheat the oven to 350°F. Grease a 9 × 5-inch loaf pan with cooking spray.

2. In a medium bowl, whisk together the flour, baking soda, and salt.

3. In a large bowl, add the mashed bananas, peanut butter, and melted butter and stir to combine. Add the brown sugar, egg, and vanilla and stir until smooth.

4. Add the dry ingredients to the wet and stir to just combine, being careful not to overmix. Pour into the prepared pan.

5. Bake for 50 to 65 minutes, or until a knife inserted into the center comes out clean and the bread springs back when lightly touched with a fingertip.

6. Transfer the bread to a cooling rack and let it cool in the pan for 10 minutes. Then run a knife around the edges and turn the bread out onto the cooling rack. Turn it right-side up and serve it slightly warm or at room temperature.

HAPPINESS IS A CHOCOLATE CHUNK COOKIE

THESE COOKIES ARE BIGGER THAN CHRISTOPHER'S HAND, but they're the first thing he reaches for from his mom's truck for good reason. Semi-sweet chocolate chunks and a perfectly chewy cookie will have you and your family reaching for more from the first bite.

Makes 24 large cookies

1 cup unsalted butter (2 sticks), melted
1 cup granulated sugar
1½ cups brown sugar
2 teaspoons kosher salt
2 large eggs
2 cups all-purpose flour
1 teaspoon baking soda
8 ounces favorite chocolate, coarsely chopped

1. In a large bowl, add the melted butter, both sugars, and salt and mix to form a smooth paste. Add the eggs and stir to combine.

2. In a medium bowl, add the flour and baking soda and whisk to combine. Add this mixture to the butter-sugar mixture and stir until just combined, being careful not to overmix the dough. Fold in the chocolate.

3. Place the bowl with the dough in the freezer for 30 minutes, or refrigerate overnight up to 4 days.

4. When ready to bake, preheat the oven to 370°F. Line two baking sheets with parchment paper.

5. Scoop balls of dough (roughly 3 tablespoons at a time) onto the prepared baking sheets, spacing them 2 inches apart.

6. Bake for 12 to 15 minutes, until golden brown and set around the edges. Remove from the oven, let cool on the baking sheets for a few minutes, then transfer to wire cooling racks to cool completely.

ORANGE-CHOCOLATE SWEETHEART COOKIES

>>>>>>>>>> <<<<<<<<<<

WITH COOKIES THIS INCREDIBLE, it's no wonder that whipping them up brought Lizzie and Ricky together. Orange zest and cinnamon make ordinary chocolate-chip cookies extraordinary. But you'll have to get the dough in the oven rather than throwing it at your baking partner if you'd like to actually eat one.

Makes 36 cookies

1 cup unsalted butter (2 sticks), softened
¾ cup granulated sugar
¾ cup packed brown sugar
2 large eggs, at room temperature
1 tablespoon orange zest
1 teaspoon vanilla extract
3½ cups all-purpose flour
1½ teaspoons baking soda
1¼ teaspoons ground cinnamon
¾ teaspoon kosher salt
2 cups semisweet chocolate chips
1 cup chopped walnuts (optional)

1. In a large bowl with an electric mixer, cream together the butter and both sugars until light and fluffy. Beat in the eggs one at a time followed by the orange zest and vanilla.

2. In a medium bowl, add the flour, baking soda, cinnamon, and salt and whisk to combine. Add to the butter-sugar mixture and beat to combine. Fold in the chocolate chips and walnuts, if using. Cover and chill in the refrigerator for 2 hours.

3. When ready to bake, preheat the oven to 375°F. Line three baking sheets with parchment paper.

4. Remove the dough from the refrigerator. Scoop balls of dough (roughly 2 tablespoons each) onto the prepared baking sheets, spacing them 2 inches apart.

5. Bake for 12 to 14 minutes, until golden brown and set around the edges. Remove from the oven, let cool on the baking sheets for a few minutes, then transfer to wire cooling racks to cool completely.

STUCK TOGETHER
STICKY BUNS

→→→→→→→→→ ←←←←←←←←←

LIKE THE LADIES OF THE VIRGIN RIVER SEWING CIRCLE, these buns stick together. And whipping up this edible quilt of cinnamon, pecans, butter, and brown sugar is far more rewarding than stirring up drama.

Makes 12 buns

FOR THE BUNS
1 (¼-ounce) package active dry yeast
¾ cup water, warm (110–115°F)
¾ cup 2% milk, warm (110–115°F)
¼ cup granulated sugar
3 tablespoons vegetable oil, plus more for greasing
2 teaspoons kosher salt
3¾–4¼ cups all-purpose flour, plus more for rolling

FOR THE FILLING
4 tablespoons unsalted butter, softened
¼ cup granulated sugar
1 tablespoon ground cinnamon
¾ cup packed brown sugar
½ cup heavy cream
1 cup coarsely chopped pecans

1. To make the buns: In a large bowl, stir together the yeast and warm water and wait until the yeast fully dissolves, about 5 minutes. Add the warm milk, granulated sugar, oil, salt, and 1¼ cups of the flour. Using an electric mixer, beat on medium speed until smooth. Stir in enough of the remaining flour to form a soft dough.

2. Turn out the dough onto a lightly floured surface and knead until smooth and elastic, 6 to 8 minutes. Coat a clean bowl with oil, place the dough inside, and turn to coat. Cover and let rise in a warm place until doubled in size, about 1 hour.

3. Punch down the dough and turn it out onto a lightly floured surface. Roll it into a 12 × 18-inch rectangle.

4. To make the filling: Spread the butter over the dough, leaving a ½-inch border around the edge. In a small bowl, combine the granulated sugar and cinnamon, then sprinkle it over the butter. Starting from a long edge, roll up the dough, then pinch the seam closed. Cut the roll into 12 equal slices.

5. Grease a 9 × 13-inch baking pan with oil. In a small bowl, stir together the brown sugar and cream. Pour into the prepared pan and sprinkle with the pecans. Place the rolls on top, cut-side down. Cover with plastic wrap and let them rise until doubled in size, 1 hour.

6. Preheat the oven to 350°F. Bake the rolls for 30 to 35 minutes or until golden brown. Let them cool in the pan for a few minutes, then invert them onto a serving plate.

DON'T KNOCK IT COCONUT CUPCAKES

You can celebrate your birthday any way you like, but you won't be sorry you included Mel's favorite coconut-infused chocolate cupcake in your special day. If you can add a hot bath and an even hotter love interest to the mix, even better!

Makes 12 cupcakes

FOR THE CUPCAKES
1 cup cake flour
½ cup cocoa powder
1 teaspoon baking powder
¼ teaspoon baking soda
¼ teaspoon kosher salt
2 large eggs, at room temperature
¾ cup granulated sugar
2 teaspoons vanilla extract
½ cup unsalted butter, melted
½ cup Greek-style yogurt

FOR THE FROSTING
1 cup (2 sticks) unsalted butter, softened
4 cups confectioners' sugar
2–3 tablespoons coconut milk
1 teaspoon coconut extract
White chocolate shavings (optional)

1. To make the cupcakes: Preheat the oven to 350°F. Fit a muffin tin with cupcake liners.

2. In a medium bowl, whisk together the flour, cocoa powder, baking powder, baking soda, and salt.

3. In another bowl, whisk the eggs, then whisk in the sugar. Add the vanilla, melted butter, and yogurt and whisk to combine. Fold in the dry ingredients and stir to combine.

4. Divide the batter among the cupcake liners, filling them two-thirds full. Bake for 15 to 20 minutes, or until a knife inserted into the center comes out clean. Let them cool for 5 minutes in the pan, then transfer them to a wire rack to cool completely before frosting.

5. To make the frosting: In a large bowl with an electric mixer, beat the butter until creamy and fluffy. Add 2 cups of the confectioners' sugar and beat to combine. Add the remaining 2 cups of sugar and beat again. Beat in the coconut milk and coconut extract until light and fluffy.

6. Transfer the frosting to a piping bag fitted with a round or star tip and frost the cooled cupcakes. If desired, sprinkle with the white chocolate shavings.

SUMMERY STRAWBERRY SHORTCAKES

→→→→→→→→→ ←←←←←←←←←

BAKING FOR FRIENDS IS ONE OF THE BEST SIMPLE PLEASURES IN LIFE—and it's a great way to keep Muriel occupied in between acting jobs. These strawberry shortcakes are so simple to whip up that you can have them whenever the mood strikes.

Makes 6 shortcakes

- 2 pints ripe strawberries, hulled and quartered
- ¾ cup sugar, divided
- 4 cups all-purpose flour, plus more for rolling
- ¼ teaspoon kosher salt
- 5 teaspoons baking powder
- 1 cup (2 sticks) unsalted butter, softened and divided
- 3 cups heavy cream, divided
- ¼ teaspoon pure vanilla extract

1. Add 1 cup of the strawberries to a large bowl and crush them. Add the remaining strawberries and ½ cup of the sugar and stir to combine. Cover with plastic wrap and set aside for 30 minutes to macerate.

2. Preheat the oven to 450°F. In a large bowl, sift together the flour, remaining ¼ cup of sugar, salt, and baking powder. Work in ¾ cup of the softened butter using a pastry cutter or two forks until it becomes crumbly. Add 1¼ cups of the cream and blend to form a soft dough.

3. Turn out the dough onto a lightly floured surface and knead for 1 minute. Roll it out to ½ inch thick, then use a 3-inch cookie cutter to cut out rounds. Gather the dough and reroll it to cut out more rounds. You should get 12 rounds.

4. Line a baking sheet with parchment paper. Place half of the rounds on the prepared baking sheet. Melt the remaining ¼ cup of butter and brush the rounds on the baking sheet with it, then place the remaining rounds on top.

5. Bake for 10 to 15 minutes until golden brown. Remove the shortcakes from the oven and separate them. Brush the insides with more of the melted butter.

6. In a medium bowl with an electric mixer, beat the remaining 1¾ cups of cream until slightly thickened. Add the vanilla and beat until it creates soft peaks. Transfer the whipped cream to a piping bag fitted with a round or star tip.

7. Place the bottom half of a shortcake on each plate. Pipe a swirl of whipped cream on each and top with a large spoonful of the strawberries. Cover with the top half, add another dollop of cream, and place a few more strawberries on top.

ALL'S FAIRE APRICOT ALMOND CAKE

LIGHT, FLUFFY, AND TOPPED WITH LUSCIOUS APRICOTS, this traditional almond cake will be the hit of your Renaissance faire (or dinner party). It makes a delightful companion to a glass of mead and—if you ask Denny—a bit of conversation with a new crush.

Serves 8

Cooking spray
1 cup all-purpose flour
½ cup almond flour
½ cup sugar
1½ teaspoons baking powder
½ teaspoon kosher salt
¾ cup unsweetened plain almond milk
1 teaspoon apple cider vinegar
½ cup olive oil
½ teaspoon almond extract
1 (15-ounce) can apricot halves in heavy syrup, drained
1 tablespoon apricot preserves
1 teaspoon hot water

1. Preheat the oven to 350°F. Coat a 9-inch springform pan with cooking spray.

2. In a large bowl, add both flours, sugar, baking powder, and salt and whisk to combine. Add the milk, vinegar, oil, and almond extract and stir until well combined, at least 2 minutes. Scrape the batter into the prepared pan. Arrange the apricots, cut-side up, on top of the batter. Bake for 30 minutes.

3. Meanwhile, in a small bowl, add the apricot preserves and hot water and whisk to combine.

4. Remove the pan from the oven, brush the cake (but not the apricots) with the glaze, and bake for 10 to 15 minutes longer, until golden on top and a knife inserted into the center comes out clean.

5. Transfer the pan to a wire rack and let it cool for 10 minutes. Remove the sides of the pan and let the cake cool on the wire rack for 30 more minutes before serving.

MEMORY-JOGGING HERMIT COOKIES

→→→→→→→→→→ ←←←←←←←←←←

THERE'S NO NEED TO TEST YOUR MEMORY WHEN GOOGLE AND SCRUMPTIOUS COOKBOOKS LIKE THIS ONE EXIST! Much like Hope herself, these old-fashioned cookies contain a bit of spice to balance their sweetness. Bake them up in traditional bars or in regular rounds.

Makes 36 cookies

1¾ cups all-purpose flour
½ teaspoon baking soda
½ teaspoon fine salt
¼ teaspoon ground nutmeg
¾ teaspoon ground cinnamon
Pinch of ground cloves
4 tablespoons vegetable shortening
4 tablespoons unsalted butter, softened
1 cup packed brown sugar
1 large egg
¼ cup brewed coffee, cold
1½ cups chopped dates or raisins
½ cup chopped walnuts or pecans

1. Preheat the oven to 375°F. Line two baking sheets with parchment paper.

2. In a medium bowl, add the flour, baking soda, salt, nutmeg, cinnamon, and cloves and whisk to combine.

3. In a large bowl with an electric mixer, add the vegetable shortening, butter, and brown sugar and beat until light and fluffy. Add the egg and cold coffee and beat on low speed until combined. Slowly add the flour mixture and beat on low speed until combined and creamy. Fold in the dates and walnuts.

4. Drop the dough by rounded teaspoon on the prepared baking sheets, spacing them 2 inches apart. Bake the cookies for 8 to 10 minutes, until golden brown and set around the edges.

5. Let the cookies cool on the pan for a few minutes, then transfer them to wire rack to cool completely.

STRAWBERRY CHEESECAKE BETWEEN FRIENDS

MURIEL KNOWS THERE'S NOTHING LIKE HOMEMADE STRAWBERRY CHEESECAKE AND SOME BACKGAMMON to take Doc's mind off things after Hope's accident. This recipe adds orange liqueur to the strawberry glaze for the ultimate treat.

Serves 8

FOR THE STRAWBERRY GLAZE

1 tablespoon cornstarch

2 tablespoons water

1 (6-ounce) jar strawberry jelly

1½ tablespoons orange-flavored liqueur or lemon juice

1 pint fresh strawberries, halved

FOR THE CHEESECAKE

2 (8-ounce packages) cream cheese, softened

½ cup plus 2 tablespoons sugar

1½ teaspoons lemon juice

1 teaspoon vanilla extract

2 large eggs, at room temperature

1 store-bought graham cracker crust

FOR THE TOPPING

1 cup sour cream

2 tablespoons sugar

½ teaspoon pure vanilla extract

1. To make the glaze: Hours before making the cake, stir together the cornstarch and water in a saucepan over medium-high heat until smooth. Add the jelly and cook, stirring, until it melts and the glaze is thickened. Remove from the heat and stir in the liqueur. Let the glaze cool to room temperature.

2. Preheat the oven to 350°F. To make the cheesecake: In a large bowl with an electric mixer, add the cream cheese and sugar and beat until smooth. Add the lemon juice, vanilla, and eggs and beat on low speed until blended. Pour the mixture into the crust.

3. Bake for 45 to 50 minutes, until the filling wobbles slightly when tapped. Leaving the oven on, transfer the cake to a wire rack and let cool for 15 minutes.

4. To make the topping: In a large bowl, add the sour cream, sugar, and vanilla and stir to combine. Spread over the slightly cooled cheesecake and bake for 5 minutes longer. Let the cake cool on the wire rack for 1 hour. Chill it in the refrigerator until cool to the touch, then cover it with plastic wrap and refrigerate overnight.

5. Just before serving, arrange the halved strawberries on top of the cheesecake. Spoon the cool glaze generously over the top and serve immediately.

GRATEFUL PEACH COBBLER

>>>>>>>>>   <<<<<<<<<

GOOD FOOD IS A UNIVERSAL LANGUAGE, and mouthwatering peach cobbler is Shirley's way of saying "thank you" to Mel for bandaging Bert's hand. Top this one off with vanilla ice cream for an even more gratifying treat.

Serves 8

5 peaches, pitted and sliced
1¾ cups sugar, divided
½ teaspoon kosher salt, divided
6 tablespoons unsalted butter, sliced
1 cup all-purpose flour
2 teaspoons baking powder
¾ cup 2% milk
½ teaspoon ground cinnamon
Vanilla ice cream, for serving

1. Preheat the oven to 350°F. In a saucepan over medium heat, add the sliced peaches, ¾ cup of the sugar, and ¼ teaspoon of the salt and stir to combine. Cook until the sugar dissolves and the peaches release their juice, about 5 minutes. Remove the mixture from the heat.

2. Add the butter to a 9 x 13-inch baking dish and place it in the oven to melt, then remove the pan from the oven.

3. In a large bowl, add the flour, remaining 1 cup of sugar, baking powder, and remaining ¼ teaspoon of salt and whisk to combine. Add the milk and stir just until combined. Pour the mixture into the pan over the melted butter and smooth it out.

4. Spoon the peaches and their juice on top of the batter. Sprinkle with the cinnamon.

5. Bake for 38 to 40 minutes, until the batter is golden brown and the peaches are bubbling. Serve warm, topped with a scoop of vanilla ice cream, if desired.

BARBECUE-READY BLUEBERRY CRUMBLE

IF THIS BLUEBERRY CRUMBLE IS THE ONLY THING YOU KNOW HOW TO MAKE, you'll still be ahead in the baking game. It's the perfect dish to welcome cute doctors into town (or to bring to the sewing circle and enjoy while you talk about them).

Serves 8

FOR THE FILLING
24 ounces (about 2 pints) fresh blueberries
2–4 tablespoons granulated sugar
2 tablespoons all-purpose flour
1 tablespoon fresh lemon juice
Pinch of fine sea salt

FOR THE CRUMBLE TOPPING
¾ cup all-purpose flour
¾ cup old-fashioned rolled oats
¼ cup brown sugar
¼ cup granulated sugar
⅛ teaspoon fine sea salt
½ cup (1 stick) unsalted butter, melted

1. Preheat the oven to 375°F.

2. To make the filling: In a large bowl, add the blueberries, granulated sugar (to taste), flour, lemon juice, and salt and toss to coat. Pour the mixture into a 2-quart baking dish.

3. To make the topping: In a medium bowl, add the flour, oats, brown sugar, granulated sugar, and salt and whisk to combine. Add the melted butter and stir until everything is moistened and the topping is crumbly. Sprinkle this mixture over the blueberry filling.

4. Bake 25 to 35 minutes until the topping is golden brown and the juices are bubbling. Let the crumble cool for 10 minutes before serving.

FLOURLESS CHOCOLATE CAKE

>>>>>>>>> <<<<<<<<<

As Mel learns from living in Virgin River, there's sweetness in simplicity. This fudgy flourless cake hits the spot with no frills. If you don't have a springform pan, just use extra parchment paper to create "wings" for easy lifting.

Serves 10

4 ounces good-quality bittersweet chocolate, chopped

½ cup (1 stick) unsalted butter

¾ cup sugar

3 large eggs

½ cup unsweetened cocoa powder

1. Preheat the oven to 375°F. Butter an 8-inch springform pan. Line the bottom with a round of parchment paper and butter the paper.

2. In a double boiler or metal mixing bowl set over a saucepan of barely simmering water, melt the chocolate and butter, stirring, until smooth. Remove the mixture from the heat, add the sugar, and whisk to combine. Whisk in the eggs one at a time, then sift in the cocoa powder. Whisk until just combined. Pour the batter into the prepared pan.

3. Bake in the middle of the oven for 25 minutes, until the top has formed a thin crust.

4. Transfer the cake to a wire rack and let it cool in the pan for 10 minutes. (The cake will sink a little in the center.) Remove the sides of the pan and transfer the cake to a serving plate.

STAR-CROSSED CHOCOLATE CAKE

>>>>>>>>>>   <<<<<<<<<<

When you're facing challenges in love like Lizzie and Ricky, take Lyddie's advice and let this incredible cake do the talking. The coffee is as sneaky as two teenage sweethearts: it brings out that rich, chocolatey goodness without a trace of coffee flavor.

Serves 12

FOR THE CAKE
Unsalted butter, for greasing
1¾ cups all-purpose flour, spooned and leveled
¾ cup unsweetened natural cocoa powder
1¾ cups granulated sugar
2 teaspoons baking soda
1 teaspoon baking powder
1 teaspoon kosher salt
2 teaspoons espresso powder
½ cup vegetable oil
2 large eggs, at room temperature
2 teaspoons vanilla extract
1 cup buttermilk, at room temperature
1 cup strong, freshly brewed hot coffee

FOR THE FROSTING
1¼ cups (2½ sticks) unsalted butter, at room temperature
3½ cups confectioners' sugar
¾ cup unsweetened cocoa powder
3–5 tablespoons heavy cream, at room temperature
¼ teaspoon kosher salt
1 teaspoon pure vanilla extract

1. Preheat the oven to 350°F. Grease two 9-inch cake pans, line each with parchment paper, then grease the parchment paper.

2. To make the cake: Whisk together the flour, cocoa powder, sugar, baking soda, baking powder, salt, and espresso powder in a large bowl.

3. In another large bowl, whisk together the oil, eggs, and vanilla. Whisk in the buttermilk until combined. Add the wet ingredients to the dry, then add the hot coffee and whisk until combined. Divide the batter between the cake pans.

4. Bake for 23 to 26 minutes or until a knife inserted into the center comes out clean. Transfer to a wire rack to cool.

5. To make the frosting: In a medium bowl with an electric mixer, beat the butter on medium speed until creamy, about 2 minutes.

6. Add the confectioners' sugar, cocoa, salt, vanilla, and 3 tablespoons of the heavy cream. Beat on low speed for 30 seconds, then increase the speed to high and beat for 1 minute. Add more confectioners' sugar to thicken the frosting or more cream to thin it.

7. Frost the top of each round, place one on top of the other, then frost the sides. Chill for at least 30 minutes before slicing and serving.

THE INGENIOUS "ESPRETZEL"

→→→→→→→→→ ←←←←←←←←←

LIZZIE IS ONTO SOMETHING WITH THIS INCREDIBLE MOCHA CREATION. Salty and sweet with a little caffeine kick, it's the perfect afternoon pick-me-up.

Serves 12

1½ cups warm water
1 (0.75-ounce) package instant yeast
1 teaspoon kosher salt
1 tablespoon brown sugar
1 tablespoon unsalted butter, melted and cooled
3¾ cups all-purpose flour, plus more for dusting
9 cups water
½ cup baking soda
¼ cup coarse sea salt
8 ounces dark or semi-sweet chocolate chips
¼ cup powdered coffee

1. Whisk the yeast into the warm water and allow it to dissolve for 1 minute. Whisk in the salt, brown sugar, and melted butter. Using a wooden spoon or mixer fitted with a dough hook, mix in 3 cups of the flour, 1 cup at a time, until the dough is thick. Slowly add the remaining ¾ cup of flour and mix just until the dough is no longer sticky and bounces back when poked.

2. Turn the dough out onto a lightly floured surface, knead for 3 minutes, and shape into a ball. Lightly cover with a towel and let rest for 10 minutes.

3. Preheat the oven to 400°F. Line two baking sheets with lightly greased parchment paper.

4. Using a sharp knife, cut the dough into twelve sections, about ⅓ cup each. Roll each section into a 20-inch-long rope. Create the pretzels by holding one end in each hand, form a circle with the dough, bringing the two ends together at the top. Twist the ends together, bring them down to rest at the bottom of the circle, and press the ends into the dough.

5. Add the water and the baking soda to a large pot and bring to a boil. Boil the pretzels one or two at a time for 20 to 30 seconds. Using a slotted spatula, lift the pretzels out of the water and let the excess water drain off. Place on the prepared baking sheets and repeat with the remaining dough.

6. Sprinkle each pretzel with sea salt, going lighter on the side you plan to dip. Then bake the pretzels for 12 to 15 minutes, until golden brown. Let cool completely on a wire rack.

7. Melt the chocolate in a microwave-safe bowl in 30-second increments. Dip one side of each pretzel into the chocolate to coat, allowing any excess to drip off, then sprinkle with a bit of coffee powder. Let the chocolate set before enjoying.

PICNIC-PERFECT LOUKOUMADES

→→→→→→→→→ ←←←←←←←←←

THERE'S NOTHING LIKE A COMMUNITY PICNIC FULL OF FOOD TRUCKS TO TEMPT YOUR TASTEBUDS! Once you try these crispy, honey-topped wonders, you'll wonder how you ever lived without them.

Makes 25 loukoumades

2 (0.25-ounce) packages active dry yeast
1 cup warm water (100°F)
½ cup warm 2% milk
¼ cup sugar
1 teaspoon kosher salt
5½ tablespoons unsalted butter, softened
3 large eggs
4 cups all-purpose flour
½ cup honey
½ cup water
4 cups vegetable oil, or as needed
2 teaspoons ground cinnamon

1. In a small bowl, sprinkle the yeast over the warm water. Let stand for 5 minutes until the yeast dissolves.

2. In a large bowl, add the warm milk, sugar, and salt and stir to dissolve. Add the yeast mixture and stir to combine.

3. Add the butter, eggs, and flour and beat with an electric mixer until it forms a smooth, soft dough. Cover the bowl and let rise in a warm place until doubled in size, 30 to 60 minutes. Stir the dough, cover, and let rise for 30 more minutes.

4. In a saucepan, add the honey and ½ cup of water and bring to a boil over medium-high heat. Stir to combine. Remove from the heat and set aside to cool.

5. Pour the oil into a large saucepan to a depth of 2 inches and heat to 350°F on a deep-fry thermometer. Line a large plate with paper towels and line a baking sheet with parchment paper.

6. With lightly oiled hands, grab about 2 tablespoons of dough, roll it into a ball, and move it to the prepared baking sheet. Repeat with the remaining dough. Working in batches, use a slotted spoon (dipped in the oil the first time) to slip the balls into the hot oil and fry until golden brown on the bottom, then turn them over to cook the other side, 2 to 3 minutes per batch. Gently place the loukoumades on the prepared plate to drain.

7. Transfer the loukoumades to a serving plate, drizzle with the honey syrup, and sprinkle with the cinnamon. Serve warm.

PRAISEWORTHY STRAWBERRY PIE

>>>>>>>>>> <<<<<<<<<<

PAIGE IS ALWAYS READY TO SING PREACHER'S PRAISES WHEN HELPING NEWCOMERS SEE THE BEST IN VIRGIN RIVER. And Preacher is quick to return the favor when it comes to Paige's pies, calling this sweet, lattice-topped treat a town favorite. One bite and you'll understand why!

Serves 8

1 (14.1-ounce) package pie crusts
  OR 2 Essential Pie Crusts (page 131)

5–6 cups fresh strawberries, hulled and sliced in half

½ cup granulated sugar, plus more for sprinkling

⅓ cup lightly packed brown sugar

¼ cup cornstarch

Large pinch of salt

2 tablespoons fresh lemon juice

Heaping ¼ teaspoon ground ginger

1. In a medium bowl, combine all the filling ingredients and toss to coat. Let macerate for 10 minutes.

2. Preheat the oven to 400°F. Line a baking sheet with parchment paper.

3. On a floured surface, roll out one crust to ⅛ inch thick and 12 inches in diameter. Press into a 9-inch pie pan and trim the edges. Pour the filling into the piecrust.

4. Roll out the second crust in the same manner. Use a pizza cutter to slice the dough into 1-inch-wide strips. Weave the strips on top of the pie, then trim and crimp the edges. Brush with the beaten egg and sprinkle with granulated sugar. Place on the prepared baking sheet.

5. Bake in the center of the oven for 15 minutes, then lower the heat to 350°F and bake for 30 minutes more, until the crust is golden and the filling is bubbling. Let cool completely before serving.

STRAWBERRY CREAM CHEESE PIE

→→→→→→→→→ ←←←←←←←←←

APOLOGIES LADEN WITH BAKED GOODS SEEM TO BE A RUNNING THEME IN *VIRGIN RIVER*—especially where Hope is concerned. Muriel deserves one, but she may not deserve this extraordinary pie.

Serves 8

1 (6-ounce) graham cracker crust OR 1 Graham Cracker Crust (page 131)

FOR THE STRAWBERRY TOPPING
5–6 cups quartered strawberries, divided
½ cup granulated sugar
2 tablespoons cornstarch
1 tablespoon lemon juice

FOR THE CREAM CHEESE LAYER
1 (8-ounce) package cream cheese, softened
½ cup powdered sugar
½ teaspoon pure vanilla extract
1 cup heavy cream

1. Preheat the oven to 375°F.

2. To make the strawberry topping: Combine 2 cups of the strawberries with the granulated sugar, cornstarch, and lemon juice in a small saucepan over medium-low heat. Cook, stirring until the strawberries release their juices, then mash the mixture until it resembles jam. Stirring constantly, bring the mixture to a boil, then continue cooking and stirring for 1 minute more. Transfer to a heat-proof bowl to cool.

3. To make the cream-cheese layer: Use an electric mixer on low to beat the cream cheese, powdered sugar, and vanilla in a medium bowl until combined.

4. In another medium bowl, beat or whisk the heavy cream on high until stiff peaks form. Gently fold into the cream-cheese mixture until combined and fluffy.

5. Spread the cream-cheese layer evenly into the pie crust and refrigerate for 10 minutes.

6. Once the strawberry mixture has cooled completely, stir in the remaining strawberries. Pour over the cream cheese, and return the pie to the refrigerator to set for at least 4 hours before serving.

DEATH BY RHUBARB PIE

→→→→→→→→→ ←←←←←←←←←

LEARN FROM BERT'S MISTAKE AND TRY TO SAVE A LITTLE ROOM FOR DESSERT WHEN THIS PIE IS LYING AROUND. It's so good, you won't be able to say no to a second slice. Luckily, the recipe is simple enough that you can whip up a backup pie in no time flat.

Serves 8

1 (14.1-ounce) package pie crusts
  OR 2 Essential Pie Crusts (page 131)
1⅓ cups sugar, plus more for sprinkling
6 tablespoons all-purpose flour
4 cups chopped rhubarb
1 tablespoon unsalted butter
1 large egg, beaten
Vanilla ice cream, for serving

1. Place an oven rack in the lowest position and preheat the oven to 450°F. Line a baking sheet with parchment paper.

2. Fit one of the pie crusts into a 9-inch pie pan and trim the edges. Use a fork to prick the bottom all over.

3. In a small bowl, combine the sugar and flour. Sprinkle one-fourth of it over the pie crust. Spoon the rhubarb on top and sprinkle with the remaining sugar mixture. Dot with the butter.

4. Cover the filling with the top crust, trimming and crimping the edges and making sure they are sealed. Using a sharp knife, cut four slits in the top crust. Brush the crust with the beaten egg and sprinkle with sugar.

5. Place the pie on the prepared baking sheet to catch any drips and bake for 15 minutes. Lower the heat to 350°F and continue baking until the filling is bubbly and the crust is golden brown, 40 to 45 minutes. Transfer to a wire rack to cool. Serve warm with a scoop of vanilla ice cream.

OLD-FASHIONED
APPLE-PEAR PIE

>>>>>>>>> <<<<<<<<<

Take it from Paige: starting over in a new place doesn't mean leaving beloved family recipes behind. Once you taste the combination of apples and pears in her signature dessert, you won't be able to go back to plain apple pie!

Serves 8

1 (14.1-ounce) package pie crusts
  OR 2 Essential Pie Crusts (page 131)
3 Granny Smith apples, peeled, cored, and sliced ½ inch thick
3 Bosc pears, peeled, cored, and sliced ½ inch thick
⅓ cup all-purpose flour
⅓ cup plus 1 tablespoon sugar, divided
2 teaspoons ground cinnamon, divided
Juice of ½ lemon
¼ teaspoon kosher salt
1 large egg, beaten

1. Preheat the oven to 375°F. Line a baking sheet with parchment paper.

2. Fit one crust into a 9-inch pie pan and trim the edges. Use a fork to prick the bottom all over.

3. In a large bowl, add the apples, pears, flour, ⅓ cup of the sugar, 1½ teaspoons of the cinnamon, lemon juice, and salt and toss to coat. Spoon it into the pie shell.

4. Fit the second crust on top of the filling. Trim and crimp the edges using your fingers or a fork, making sure they are sealed. Using a sharp knife, cut four slits in the top crust.

5. In a small bowl, combine the remaining 1 tablespoon sugar and remaining ½ teaspoon cinnamon. Brush the crust with the beaten egg and sprinkle with cinnamon-sugar mixture.

6. Cover the crust edges with strips of foil to prevent burning. Place the pie on the prepared baking sheet and bake for 25 minutes. Remove the foil and continue baking until the fruit is tender and the liquid is bubbling, about 50 more minutes. Transfer to a wire rack to cool for 20 minutes before serving.

MAKE LEMON MERINGUE PIE OUT OF LEMONS

→→→→→→→→→ ←←←←←←←←←

If there's one thing the residents of Virgin River know how to do, it's how to turn bitter moments into something sweet. What better way to celebrate that spirit than with a deliciously sweet-tart pie like this one?

Serves 8

1 (14-ounce) package pie crusts OR 1 Essential Pie Crust (page 131)

FOR THE FILLING

1 cup sugar

5 tablespoons cornstarch

½ teaspoon kosher salt

½ cup fresh lemon juice

1½ cups water

4 large egg yolks

3 tablespoons unsalted butter, diced

2 teaspoons lemon zest

FOR THE MERINGUE

5 large egg whites, at room temperature

¾ cup sugar

¼ teaspoon cream of tartar

Pinch kosher salt

½ teaspoon pure vanilla extract

1. Roll one pie crust out to be 13 inches in diameter. (Save the other for another recipe.) Gently press the crust into a 9-inch pie plate and refrigerate it for another 2 hours.

2. Preheat the oven to 375°F. Trim away any excess crust, then crimp the edges. Use a fork to prick the bottom of the crust all over. Lay a sheet of parchment paper inside the crust, fill it with pie weights, and bake it for 10 minutes. Then carefully remove the parchment and weights and continue baking until the edges are deep golden brown and the center is lightly golden, 10 to 12 minutes more. Let the crust cool completely.

3. To make the filling: Whisk together the sugar, cornstarch, and salt in a medium saucepan, then whisk in the lemon juice and water. Gently whisk the mixture over medium heat until thick and bubbling.

4. Whisk the egg yolks in a medium bowl. Gradually whisk in half of the hot sugar mixture, then add the yolk mixture back into the saucepan. Bring the mixture to a simmer and cook, stirring constantly with a rubber spatula, for 1 minute.

5. Remove the mixture from the heat and stir in the butter and lemon zest until completely incorporated. Pour the finished filling directly into the pie crust. Cover it with plastic wrap pressed directly against the surface of the filling, and transfer it to the refrigerator.

6. To make the meringue: Use a hand or stand mixer fitted with a whisk attachment to combine the egg whites, sugar, cream of tartar, and salt in a large, heatproof bowl. In a double-boiler, whisk the meringue by hand until the sugar dissolves and the mixture feels hot to the touch. Remove the bowl from the heat and whisk in the vanilla on medium-high. Continue until stiff peaks form.

7. Remove the plastic wrap from the pie and gently cover the filling with meringue, creating soft swirls and peaks. Broil the meringue in the oven just until peaks are golden brown. Refrigerate the pie until completely cool and set, about 4 hours.

NO LIES, JUST PECAN PIE

→→→→→→→→→ ←←←←←←←←

WITH PIES LIKE THIS ONE IN THE WORLD, it's no wonder that Paige has a weakness for pecans. You will, too, once you taste this pie's incredible, caramelized filling. And you can't get caught in a lie like she does if you're busy chewing!

Serves 8

1 (14.1-ounce) package pie crusts OR
  1 Essential Pie Crust (page 131)
3 large eggs
1 cup sugar
¼ teaspoon kosher salt
½ cup light corn syrup
½ cup dark corn syrup
4 tablespoons unsalted butter, melted
1 tablespoon vanilla extract
1¼ cups (5 ounces) pecan halves

Whipped cream, for serving (optional)

1. Place a rack in the bottom third of the oven and preheat the oven to 350°F.

2. On a lightly floured surface, roll out one crust into a 13-inch round. (Save the other for another recipe.) Fit it into a 9-inch glass pie dish and trim the edge to ½ inch. Fold the edge under itself and crimp with your fingers or a fork. Refrigerate for 30 minutes.

3. In a medium bowl, add the eggs, sugar, and salt and whisk to combine. Add the corn syrups, butter, and vanilla and stir to combine. Stir in the pecans.

4. Pour the filling into the pie shell and adjust the pecans to form a decorative pattern, if desired. Cover the edges with foil strips to prevent burning.

5. Bake for 50 minutes, or until the crust is golden and the filling has expanded but is not completely set. Remove the foil strips, transfer to a wire rack, and let cool completely. Serve with a dollop of whipped cream, if desired.

PIE CRUST FROM SCRATCH

When you want to go the extra mile, whip up your pie crust from scratch. The Essential Pie Crust is perfect for fruit and nut pies—just double the recipe for a double-crust pie. The Graham Cracker Crust pairs perfectly with pudding- and cream cheese–based pies.

Makes 1 pie crust

ESSENTIAL PIE CRUST

1 cup all-purpose flour, plus more for rolling
½ teaspoon kosher salt
½ teaspoon sugar
½ cup (1 stick) cold unsalted butter, cut into ½-inch cubes
¼ cup ice water

1. In a food processor, pulse the flour with the salt and sugar. Add the butter and pulse until the size of small peas. Sprinkle with the ice water and pulse just until the crumbs are evenly moistened.

2. Turn out the dough onto a lightly floured work surface and form into a ball. Flatten into a disk, wrap in plastic, and refrigerate for at least 30 minutes.

Makes 1 pie crust

GRAHAM CRACKER CRUST

1½ cups graham cracker crumbs
2 tablespoons granulated sugar
1 tablespoon packed brown sugar
7 tablespoons unsalted butter, melted

1. Combine the graham cracker crumbs and sugars in a medium bowl. Stir in the melted butter until well combined.

2. Pour the mixture into a 9-inch pie pan and use the bottom of a glass to press the crumbs into the bottom of the pan and up the sides. Chill in the refrigerator for 10 to 20 minutes.

CONVERSION CHARTS

Metric and Imperial Conversions

(These conversions are rounded for convenience)

Ingredient	Cups/Tablespoons/Teaspoons	Ounces	Grams/Milliliters
Butter	1 cup/16 tablespoons/2 sticks	8 ounces	230 grams
Cheese, shredded	1 cup	4 ounces	110 grams
Cornstarch	1 tablespoon	0.3 ounce	8 grams
Cream cheese	1 tablespoon	0.5 ounce	14.5 grams
Flour, all-purpose	1 cup/1 tablespoon	4.5 ounces/0.3 ounce	125 grams/8 grams
Flour, whole wheat	1 cup	4 ounces	120 grams
Fruit, dried	1 cup	4 ounces	120 grams
Fruits or veggies, chopped	1 cup	5 to 7 ounces	145 to 200 grams
Fruits or veggies, pureed	1 cup	8.5 ounces	245 grams
Honey, maple syrup, or corn syrup	1 tablespoon	0.75 ounce	20 grams
Liquids: cream, milk, water, or juice	1 cup	8 fluid ounces	240 milliliters
Oats	1 cup	5.5 ounces	150 grams
Salt	1 teaspoon	0.2 ounce	6 grams
Spices: cinnamon, cloves, ginger, or nutmeg (ground)	1 teaspoon	0.2 ounce	5 milliliters
Sugar, brown, firmly packed	1 cup	7 ounces	200 grams
Sugar, white	1 cup/1 tablespoon	7 ounces/0.5 ounce	200 grams/12.5 grams
Pure vanilla extract	1 teaspoon	0.2 ounce	4 grams

Oven Temperatures

Temperature	Celsius	Gas Mark
225°	110°	¼
250°	120°	½
275°	140°	1
300°	150°	2
325°	160°	3
350°	180°	4
375°	190°	5
400°	200°	6
425°	220°	7
450°	230°	8

INDEX